S0-BVJ-431

PRAYING EFFECTIVELY

Bennie S. Triplett

PRAYING
EFFECTIVELY

Bible Studies
in
Prayer

Scripture quotations are taken from the following sources: *The Holy Bible, New King James Version (NKJV)*, Copyright © 1979, 1980, 1982 by Thomas Nelson, Inc., Nashville, TN. Used by permission. *The Living Bible (TLB)*, Copyright © 1971 by Tyndale House Publishers, Wheaton, IL. Used by permission. *American Standard Version (ASV)*, Copyright © 1901 by Thomas Nelson & Sons, Copyright © 1929 by International Council of Religious Education.

Lyric quotations are taken from the following sources: *Hymns of the Spirit*, Copyright © 1969, Pathway Press, Cleveland, TN. *Church Hymnal*, Copyright © 1951, Tennessee Music and Printing Company, Cleveland, TN.

SHUT DE DO by Randy Stonehill. Copyright © 1983 by Stonehillian Music (administered by Word Music) and Word Music (a division of Word, Inc.). All Rights Reserved. International Copyright Secured. Used by permission.

A PRAYER FOR PATIENCE. Used with permission of The Helen Steiner Rice Foundation.

DEDICATION

This book is lovingly dedicated to my wife, Helen—my life partner and also my prayer partner. It is also dedicated to our children and grandchildren—to our daughter, Rene', (deceased November 16, 1989) and her husband, Dwain Pyeatt, who for 16 years were shepherds of a growing congregation; to their children, Kelli Michelle and Jonathan Matthew; to our son, Steve, and his wife, Jean Tillery Triplett, who serve in their local church; and to their children, Bennie Stevens III and Jesse Clayton—who are all a vital part of my life and ministry.

CONTENTS

FOREWORD

Never has there been a greater need for intercessory prayer than now. The times demand a book like *Praying Effectively*. God has directed Bennie Triplett to write this book.

Christian people today are experiencing spiritual battle. "For we wrestle not against flesh and blood, but against principalities, against powers, against the rulers of the darkness of this world, against spiritual wickedness in high places" (Ephesians 6:12). We are admonished in Ephesians 6:18, "Praying always with all prayer and supplication in the Spirit, and watching thereunto with all perseverance and supplication for all saints."

Bennie Triplett is fully qualified to author such a book on *How to Pray*. The circumstances of his early life prepared him to know the value of prayer. His many years of experience as an evangelist, pastor, state overseer, state youth director, program director of Forward in Faith, chairman of Northwest Bible College Board of Directors, member of the World Missions Board, member of the Council of Twelve, and general director of radio and television have uniquely prepared him to write this book. Bennie and his wife, Helen, are living examples of what can be accomplished through prayer.

I personally urge everyone to take advantage of his excellent advice on prayer. It is important to pray intelligently and directly to the Lord of the universe. Those who pray in faith will be effective, especially when their united prayers are unceasingly offered to our heavenly Father. Reverence and fervency will form the basis for earnest prayer as we learn to meditate before the Lord and to patiently await God's answer.

I commend Bennie Triplett for having the insight, burden and concern to author this much-needed book.

Raymond E. Crowley

PREFACE

These studies were born out of the urgency of the times, a great need in my own personal life and a void in the lives of those for whom I was spiritually responsible. I am thoroughly convinced that nothing of real significance happens in the kingdom of God except through sincere prayer.

Some of these messages have been used to set the stage for revivals, camp meetings and crusades. Others were used on prayer meeting nights in the local pastorate to plant the seeds for an undergirding, ongoing prayer ministry in the Body. Some were devotionals shared in homes, small groups or hospitals and mailed out as a tract to those who requested it.

This particular series began my second tenure with Forward in Faith, the radio and television ministry I helped to establish in 1958. It also inspired the beginning of Home Prayer Warriors, the worldwide intercessory prayer ministry of *Forward in Faith*.

The thesis of these messages is simple and to the point. First and foremost, Jesus teaches us *to pray*, and then He teaches us *how to pray*. Similar to many lessons in life, we learn to pray by praying. There are many results and rewards in the ministry of prayer which are not readily apparent in routine Christian service. Prayer is multidimensional. The more we pray, the more we want to pray. The more we study the Word of God concerning prayer, the more we see the unending, indescribable worth of this blessed privilege.

It is hoped that these scriptural studies may be used to advance the kingdom of God. I commend them to individuals as a prayer primer to whet their spiritual appetite for more of God. Helen and I commend them to parents and family members for their own personal spiritual growth. To leaders, whose examples speak far more eloquently than words, we entrust these truths for further distribution and impartation, believing that the greatest and most fruitful days are yet ahead for those who will cry as did the disciple in Luke 11:1, "Lord, teach us to pray."

I was 26 years of age when Helen and I drove a little Studebaker car into a field on a mountain in West Virginia. The man coming from behind the International logging truck was my daddy, John Triplett. He had never seen me, and I had never seen him. Because of severe circumstances, he had left my mother seven months before I was born. A miraculous answer to prayer had finally brought us face-to-face. After a brief and dramatic visit, I explained that we must return for revival services in Troutman, North Carolina. As I was driving out through the gate, he said to me, "By the way, this church you're preaching for, is it Mr. Freeman's church?"

"Yes," I said, "it's Grandpa Freeman's church."

"I thought so," John Triplett replied. "He was some kind of a man! Many a time I would come home and find him in the back room or out in the woodshed on his knees. He was a man of prayer."

CHAPTER

1

HOW TO
PRAY

     Prayer is the Christian's breath. He who prays not breathes not; and he who breathes not lives not. Prayer is the primary means of communication between man and God. God speaks to man through His Word. Man speaks to God through his prayers. Prayer is a beautiful and eternal privilege God has given humanity, whereby we can communicate with Divinity. Prayer is the privilege of all people everywhere. What a different world ours would be if everyone would learn to pray! Is it any wonder the disciple responded as he did in Luke 11:1, after observing Jesus in prayer with His heavenly Father? His spontaneous response was, "Lord, teach us to pray!"

Lord, Teach Us!

God and Man Together
    Man was created by God in the image and likeness of God (Genesis 1:27). God intended that God and man should always be together.

God and Man Apart
    God has never desired that He and man should be apart. The first separation came when man ceased communica-

tion with God and established dialogue with the devil in the Garden of Eden. Man's headlong plunge into iniquity began when he refused to heed the truth of God and deliberately preferred the lies of the devil (Genesis 2:16, 17; 3:1-24).

The Result of Separation

Since that day, man has continued in his evil ways (Genesis 6:5). God with man is a wonderful relationship. Man without God is a contradiction in principle to everything God created.

Lord, Teach Us!

God Is Man's Best Teacher

Who can teach man better than the One who created him—formed and fashioned him in His own likeness and in His own image? Who can teach man better than the One who loved him enough to breathe into him the breath of life and cause him to be a living soul? Who can teach man better than the One who made him lord over all creation— to have dominion over the beasts of the fields, the fowls of the air and the fish of the sea? Who can teach man better than the One who told him the truth? (And that truth came to pass exactly as it was told to man.) No greater teaching-learning relationship can exist than that between God and man. God is the source of all truth (Deuteronomy 32:4; Isaiah 65:16). Indeed Christ, the Son, is the Truth (John 14:6). The Holy Spirit is the Spirit of truth (John 14:17; 15:26; 16:13). The Bible is the Word of truth (John 17:17). All of God's promises "are yea, and in him Amen, unto the glory of God by us" (2 Corinthians 1:20). Not one promise of God is "no" to those who will believe and meet the conditions. His promises are "yes" and "so be it." In Christ the lessons of life are always positive and truthful.

God Has Man's Best Interest at Heart

From the beginning God has instructed man in the necessary truths of righteousness. When Jesus came, He was called Rabbi, Master and Teacher. When the Holy Spirit came, His mission was to "guide . . . [us] into all truth" (John 16:13), "teach . . . [us] all things, and bring all things to . . . [our] remembrance" (John 14:26). God has taught us and continues to teach us through His Word. "All scripture is given by inspiration of God, and is profitable for doctrine, for reproof, for correction, for instruction in righteousness: that the man of God may be perfect, throughly furnished unto all good works" (2 Timothy 3:16, 17).

God Is Not the Problem

God is willing and ready to teach us! Man, however, is often not willing to be taught. The apostle Paul explained it in 2 Timothy 3:7, "Ever learning, and never able to come to the knowledge of the truth."

God, Man and Prayer

Man's relationship with God depends on the free-flowing exercise of prayer. This means keeping the lines of communication open and unobstructed. Check the record historically. Anytime you find a godly man or woman, you will in turn find a person of prayer. When I think of George Washington, our first president and the father of our country, my first reflection is not of the cherry tree but rather the mental image of the general on his knees, calling out to God in prayer in behalf of his country and his countrymen.

Check the domestic record, and the choice memories of home and family will most assuredly include sacred times, special times and prayerful times. God, man and prayer—these three are interrelated. If prayer is left out, the relationship dies. If prayer is maintained, nothing will ever be able to separate us from the love of God that is in Christ Jesus our Lord (Romans 8:38, 39).

Check the record in the Scriptures, and you will find that every great character in the Bible was also a person of prayer. Through faith, obedience and prayer power, Abraham's intercession became a powerful force with God (Genesis 18:23-32). As Jacob wrestled with God, he said, "I will not let thee go except thou bless me." After God blessed him, Jacob called the name of the place Peniel, saying, "For I have seen God face to face, and my life is preserved" (see Genesis 32:24-30). Israel was spared when Moses prayed, "If thou wilt forgive their sin—; and if not, blot me, I pray thee, out of thy book which thou hast written" (Exodus 32:32).

Hannah, in prayer, asked God for a son, and God gave her a son (1 Samuel 1:20). She named him Samuel, which means "asked of God" or "God heard." David the king was a man of prayer. In Psalm 55:16, 17, he wrote, "As for me, I will call upon God; and the Lord shall save me. Evening, and morning, and at noon, will I pray, and cry aloud: and he shall hear my voice."

A Gentile woman said to Jesus, "Lord, help me." He spoke the word and healed her daughter that very hour (Matthew 15:22-28). Jesus himself asked, "Shall not God avenge his own elect, which cry day and night unto him?" He answered, "I tell you that he will avenge them speedily" (Luke 18:7, 8). God, man and prayer have always been a powerful combination. It remains an unbeatable alliance today.

Lord, Teach Us to Pray

God Teaches Us to Pray

We need to be taught *to* pray before we are taught *how to pray.* God said in His Word: "Call unto me, and I will answer thee, and shew thee great and mighty things, which thou knowest not" (Jeremiah 33:3). "Call upon me in the day of trouble: I will deliver thee, and thou shalt glorify me" (Psalm 50:15). "He shall call upon me, and I will answer him: I will be with him in trouble; I will deliver him, and honour him" (Psalm 91:15). "And it shall come to pass, that before they call, I will answer; and while they are yet speaking, I will hear" (Isaiah 65:24). God's exhortations to pray and His eagerness to answer have been man's strongest inducement to prayer.

Jesus Teaches Us to Pray

"The harvest truly is great, but the labourers are few: pray ye therefore the Lord of the harvest, that he would send forth labourers into his harvest" (Luke 10:2). "And I say unto you, Ask, and it shall be given you; seek, and ye shall find; knock, and it shall be opened unto you" (Luke 11:9). "If ye then, being evil, know how to give good gifts unto your children: how much more shall your heavenly Father give the Holy Spirit to them that ask him?" (Luke 11:13). "Watch ye and pray, lest ye enter into temptation. The spirit truly is ready, but the flesh is weak" (Mark 14:38). "And he said unto them, This kind can come forth by nothing, but by prayer and fasting" (Mark 9:29).

Other Biblical Examples Teach Us to Pray

The Bible is replete with exhortations and examples of prayer. In Genesis 4:26, the Bible says, "Then began men to call upon the name of the Lord." Thus the birth date of prayer is recorded in sacred Scripture. It was a dark antediluvian night which brought it forth. Since that original hour, many men have prayed.

Abraham "called upon the name of the Lord" (Genesis

12:8). His prayer saved Lot and his family from the destruction which fell upon Sodom and Gomorrah (Genesis 19:28, 29). Again he prayed, and the first recorded healing was in answer to Abraham's prayer (Genesis 20:17).

Isaac prayed, and Rebekah, who had been barren, conceived (Genesis 25:21).

Jacob cried out, "Deliver me, I pray thee, from the hand of my brother, from the hand of Esau: for I fear him, lest he will come and smite me, and the mother with the children" (Genesis 32:11). In answer to Jacob's prayer, "Esau ran to meet him, and embraced him, and fell on his neck, and kissed him: and they wept" (Genesis 33:4).

From the dungeon Joseph prayed for deliverance. Shortly thereafter, Pharaoh said to him, "See, I have set thee over all the land of Egypt. . . . And he made him to ride in the second chariot which he had; and they cried before him, Bow the knee: and he made him ruler over all the land of Egypt" (Genesis 41:41, 43).

Moses prayed, and the waters of the Red Sea parted and became a superhighway of dry ground for the children of Israel to cross on (Exodus 14:21, 22). At Marah he prayed, and a tree cast into the bitter waters was enough to make them sweet (Exodus 15:25). From bitter waters made sweet, the children of Israel came to a place of no water. Moses cried unto the Lord, and God sent water out of the smitten rock (Exodus 17:1-6).

Joshua, successor to Moses, gained a country, united a people and watched the walls of Jericho fall flat, after he fell on his face to the earth in prayer (Joshua 7:6).

Samson, the Hercules of the Bible, became weak in the presence of a pretty woman. Chained, dismayed and blinded by the hands of his enemies, he prayed, "Lord God, remember me, I pray thee, and strengthen me, I pray thee, only this once, O God, that I may be at once avenged of the Philistines for my two eyes" (Judges 16:28). And 3,000 Philistines were crushed to death.

Hannah, on her knees in the tabernacle at Shiloh, begged God to fulfill the longing of her heart. "And she vowed a vow, and said, O Lord of hosts, if thou wilt indeed look on the affliction of thine handmaid, and remember me, and not forget thine handmaid, but wilt give unto thine handmaid a man child, then I will give him unto the Lord all the days of his life" (1 Samuel 1:11). When the child was born, Hannah said, "For this child I prayed; and the Lord hath given me my petition which I asked of him" (1 Samuel 1:27).

It was also said of David that he "enquired of the Lord" (1 Samuel 23:2). While only a youth, David had come against Goliath in the name of the Lord and had prevailed over him, with a sling and a stone (1 Samuel 17:40-50).

David declared in Psalm 145:18, "The Lord is nigh unto all them that call upon him, to all that call upon him in truth." And he pledged in Psalm 5:3, "My voice shalt thou hear in the morning, O Lord; in the morning will I direct my prayer unto thee, and will look up."

"Let my prayer be set forth before thee as incense; and the lifting up of my hands as the evening sacrifice" (Psalm 141:2). "I remember thee upon my bed, and meditate on thee in the night watches" (Psalm 63:6).

Elijah prayed at Mount Carmel in public, and God answered by fire and brought revival to a nation.

Thank God for the exhortations and examples that teach us to pray! How inspiring, how practical and how all-encompassing the scope and details of supplication found in the Word of God are! It is as if the Holy Spirit knew the things each generation would encounter and spared no effort in making sure each of us would be built up in the most holy faith.

Teach Us as John Also Taught His Disciples

Whatever John the Baptist taught his disciples, you can rest assured he taught them only the things he had seen and heard. How is it that a person such as John the Baptist would know to pray and how to teach others to pray? The answer is quite obvious when you study the background of the "wilderness wonder." His miraculous birth, the life and ministry of his father, Zacharias, and the dedication of his mother, Elizabeth, all contributed to the shaping of his unique premessianic personality. Whatever he taught his disciples about prayer he surely learned from his parents.

His father, Zacharias, was a Jewish priest who served faithfully in the Temple. He was married to Elizabeth, a devout woman of "like precious faith." She was doubly blessed in that she was the daughter of a priest and the wife of a priest. Her only sorrow was that she was barren. Now advanced in years, Zacharias and his wife had prayed for a child most of their lives. While carrying out his Temple duties, he was chosen for the special task of entering into the inner sanctuary to burn incense before the Lord while the people gathered in prayer outside.

Suddenly the archangel Gabriel appeared before the altar of incense. Zacharias was startled. The angel said, "Don't be afraid, Zacharias, for I have come to tell you that God has heard your prayer. Your wife, Elizabeth, will bear you a son, and you are to name him John. He will be one of the Lord's great men and will be filled with the Holy Spirit, even before his birth! He will persuade many to turn to the Lord God" (Luke 1:13-16, *paraphrased*).

Elizabeth was overjoyed at her pregnancy. "How kind the Lord is," she exclaimed, "to take away my disgrace of having no children!" Now Elizabeth was the kinsman of Mary, a young virgin and a descendant of King David, who also was visited by the angel Gabriel. Mary had been chosen to be the mother of Jesus, the Messiah. The news was so thrilling she journeyed immediately to the house of Zacharias and Elizabeth. Upon entering the house, she called out a greeting. When Elizabeth heard Mary's voice, the baby leaped for joy in Elizabeth's womb, and she was filled with the Holy Ghost and prophesied concerning Mary's divine destiny. The meeting of these two godly ladies is one of the most poignant scenes in all sacred Scripture (Luke 1:25-56).

John the Baptist was a product of prayer. His parents were people of prayer. The angel had told Zacharias that John would be a man of rugged spirit and power like Elijah, who was a prophet of prayer. It was further announced that he would be the forerunner of Jesus and prepare the way for the coming of the Messiah. He would move fathers to love their children and convert rebellious sons to the ways of the Lord (Luke 1:17). Indeed, John the Baptist knew the value of prayer. It was a part of the total chemistry of his being. It is not surprising, therefore, that Christ's disciples asked Him to teach them as "John also taught his disciples."

Lord, Teach Us!

The very fact that one of the disciples asked Him to teach them is evidence that Jesus had already been teaching. The inquiring disciple came very close to interrupting the Lord during His prayer as though he could hardly wait. Luke did say "when he ceased" in fairness to the eager listener. The words "as He was praying" let us in on the dynamics of the occasion. The spiritual palates of the apostles had already been sufficiently teased. The seeds of precept and example had already been planted and were now coming forth in a spontaneity which exclaimed, "Lord, teach us!"

Jesus Teaches Us by Precept

Jesus said, "Pray ye" (Matthew 6:9), "Pray ye therefore" (9:38), and "Pray always" (Luke 21:36). He also advised, "Pray for them which despitefully use you, and persecute you" (Matthew 5:44). In Matthew 6:9 He introduced His model prayer with this admonition: "After this manner therefore pray ye." In Matthew 26:41 He exhorted, "Watch and pray." In Mark 11:24, 25 He alluded to the inclusiveness and sacredness of prayer in these terms: "What things soever ye desire, when ye pray, believe that ye receive them, and ye shall have them. And when ye stand praying, forgive." Jesus taught by advice, rule, command and instruction.

Jesus Teaches Us by Example

One of the most forceful statements by Jesus is "I pray." It is found several times in John 17. It sets Jesus apart as the Great Intercessor, as the supreme pattern and example for all men and women in all ages to follow. Notice His words: "I go and pray yonder" (Matthew 26:36); "I will pray the Father" (John 14:16); "I pray not that thou shouldest take them out of the world" (John 17:15); "Neither pray I for these alone" (John 17:20). His three and a half years of ministry were a model of prayer.

Jesus teaches us to pray privately. "And when he had sent the multitudes away, he went up into a mountain apart to pray: and when the evening was come, he was there alone" (Matthew 14:23). "Then cometh Jesus with them unto a place called Gethsemane, and saith unto the disciples, Sit ye here, while I go and pray yonder" (Matthew 26:36). "And in the morning, rising up a great while before day, he went out, and departed into a solitary place, and there prayed" (Mark 1:35). "And he withdrew himself into the wilderness, and prayed" (Luke 5:16). "And it came to pass in those days, that he went out into a mountain to pray, and continued all night in prayer to God" (Luke 6:12). "And it came to pass, as he was alone praying, his disciples were with him: and he asked them, saying, Whom say the people that I am?" (Luke 9:18).

Jesus teaches us to pray publicly. "At that time [while speaking to the multitudes in the cities] Jesus answered and said, I thank thee, O Father, Lord of heaven and earth, because thou hast hid these things from the wise and prudent, and hast revealed them unto babes" (Matthew 11:25). "And as they were eating, Jesus took bread, and blessed it, and brake it, and gave it to the disciples, and said, Take, eat; this is my body" (Matthew 26:26). "And it came to pass, that, as he was praying in a certain place, when he ceased, one of his disciples said unto him, Lord, teach us to pray, as John also taught his disciples" (Luke 11:1). "Then they took away the stone from the place where the dead was laid. And Jesus lifted up his eyes, and said, Father, I thank thee that thou hast heard me" (John 11:41). "These words spake Jesus, and lifted up his eyes to heaven, and said, Father, the hour is come; glorify thy Son, that thy Son also may glorify thee" (John 17:1).

Jesus teaches us to pray for provisions. In Matthew 6:11 our Lord's Prayer includes the petition "Give us this day our daily bread." Publicly He prayed prior to the partaking of food (Matthew 14:19; Mark 6:41). Privately He prayed as others were partaking of food (Matthew 26:26).

Jesus teaches us to pray long prayers. He arose a great while before day to go to a solitary place to pray. On another occasion He continued all night in prayer to God (Luke 6:12). And in John 17, He prayed for Himself, His mission, His followers and those who would follow.

Jesus teaches us to pray short, spontaneous prayers. "And about the ninth hour Jesus cried with a loud voice, saying,

Eli, Eli, lama sabachthani? that is to say, My God, my God, why hast thou forsaken me?" (Matthew 27:46). "Then they took away the stone from the place where the dead was laid. And Jesus lifted up his eyes, and said, Father, I thank thee that thou hast heard me. And I knew that thou hearest me always: but because of the people which stand by I said it, that they may believe that thou hast sent me" (John 11:41, 42). "Now is my soul troubled; and what shall I say? Father, save me from this hour: but for this cause came I unto this hour. Father, glorify thy name. Then came there a voice from heaven, saying, I have both glorified it, and will glorify it again" (John 12:27, 28).

Jesus teaches us to pray for our friends. "Then were there brought unto him little children, that he should put his hands on them, and pray: and the disciples rebuked them" (Matthew 19:13). "But I have prayed for thee, that thy faith fail not: and when thou art converted, strengthen thy brethren" (Luke 22:32). He also prayed for His friends in John 17.

Jesus teaches us to pray for our enemies. "But I say unto you, Love your enemies, bless them that curse you, do good to them that hate you, and pray for them which despitefully use you, and persecute you" (Matthew 5:44). "Then said Jesus, Father, forgive them; for they know not what they do. And they parted his raiment, and cast lots" (Luke 23:34).

Jesus teaches us to pray for ourselves. His prayers for Himself were always with the thought of others. "And he went a little farther, and fell on his face, and prayed, saying, O my Father, if it be possible, let this cup pass from me: nevertheless not as I will, but as thou wilt" (Matthew 26:39). Any prayer for ourselves must eventually include God's will, God's glory and God's mission. *Lord, teach us.*

As in all lessons of life, we learn to pray by praying. I

must have been about 7 or 8 years old when Grandpa Freeman spotted me staring at a secondhand guitar hanging in the window of a pawn shop on East Trade Street in downtown Charlotte, North Carolina. The next thing I knew, he had scraped up enough money to purchase that guitar for me. We took it by Aunt Mable Blackmon's house in the mill village on the way home. She tuned it and showed me how to put my fingers on the strings to form three chords: C, F and G. My thumb lapped over the top of the third fret on the top string, and my second index finger hooked under the bottom on the first string. Even though I watched Aunt Mable play, listened to what she taught and read a book of instructions, I did not learn to play by looking, listening and reading alone. I learned to play by playing. We all learn to walk by walking and to eat by eating.

The story is told of fish in a beautiful stream at the bottom of Mammoth Cave in Kentucky. The fish are blind. Earlier in the life of the species they could see, but because of the darkness of the cave, they gradually ceased using their eyes, and now they are blind. Prayerless folk are either those who have never prayed or those who have ceased to pray. Prayer is similar to all other lessons of life. We learn to pray by praying. *Lord, teach us to pray!*

Prayer
Thank You, Father, that the greatest truths and the most profound lessons in life often come naturally, automatically, spontaneously and even instinctively. Thank You for the privilege of prayer. Thank You for teaching us to pray by the precept and example of Your Son, Jesus Christ. Now help us to learn, receive and respond accordingly. In Jesus' name. Amen.

CHAPTER

2

PRAYING
INTELLIGENTLY

Prayer is the greatest force in the universe. It transcends all other forces. Its power, privilege, impact and influence cannot be exaggerated even in a technological age when many forces stagger the mind and the imagination. Prayer is the most important exercise in which a Christian can engage. The older a Christian becomes, the more he is persuaded of the importance of prayer. The more one grows in grace and in the knowledge of Jesus Christ, the more he prays, the better he prays and the more he realizes the poverty of prayerlessness.

Why is it that those who apparently need prayer so little seem to pray so much, while those who obviously need prayer so much pray so little? Could many of the perplexities concerning prayer point out the widespread ignorance of the subject? And how do you explain the seeming lack of interest, considering its importance?

Chapter 1 dealt with Christ's teaching us *to* pray. This chapter begins the discussion of the *how to* process of prayer. When we reflect upon the disciple's request, "Lord, teach us to pray," we may also feel compelled to add, "Yes, Lord, and please teach us to pray intelligently."

What Do We Mean by Intelligent Praying?

Perhaps the word *intelligence* is somewhat "high-sounding" to you. However, on closer examination, you will see it is exactly the right word to describe the way we ought to pray.

Consider the concepts of these three words: *knowledge*, *wisdom* and *intelligence*.

Knowledge is information acquired, that which is learned through instruction, study or experience. The scope and depth of our knowledge has to do with the quality and discipline of our interest and energies. It can also be closely related to the motivation and example of those who instruct us.

Wisdom is understood as God-given (James 1:5). Wisdom and intelligence are closely related. To have wisdom is to have keen perception, to show sound judgment, and to be able to discern what is true and right and lasting. Often wisdom is bestowed for special tasks and purposes.

Intelligence means having the capacity to apply knowledge, to have understanding, to have the ability to apply what has been learned by experience to new situations. It is that down-to-earth, everyday common sense which helps us to use *wisdom* and *knowledge* to the best advantage.

Some exceptionally gifted individuals seem able to use their talents to great advantage, while others waste their talents through neglect and unconcern. On the other hand, some individuals with little or no natural talent, through discipline, dedication and hard work, surpass many who are gifted. We are all familiar with the proverbial out-of-touch genius who can't tie his shoelaces or who, in the words of the old-timer, "doesn't have the sense to come in out of the rain." But there is beauty in the balance of knowledge, wisdom and intelligence.

Lord, give us the common sense to take full advantage of everything You have given us. May we utilize for Your glory and honor everything You have placed at our disposal.

Jesus Taught His Disciples to Pray Intelligently

After teaching His disciples by example, Jesus began to teach them "precept upon precept; line upon line; here a little, and there a little" (Isaiah 28:10).

The Intelligent Way Is the Best Way

The word *intelligent* means to be well-versed or well-informed. Intelligence refers to the ability to effectively apply clear thinking and good judgment in any problem or situation. It means the power to reason and distinguish, to gather information and insight, and to be able to act accordingly. And that which is *intelligible* is easily understood, clearly stated, obvious, plain, clear and distinct. Now the word *intelligent* doesn't seem to be so "high-sounding" after all, does it? It is precisely the practical term we need to define how one should pray.

The Intelligent Way Is the Scriptural Way

The Bible is a most intelligent book. It is a collection of the most precise and valuable information the world has ever known. Its truths and instructions are clear and concise. Its heroes of faith seem to be the wisest, most courageous, knowledgeable, honorable, gentle, souls who ever lived. The Bible is the greatest how-to encyclopedia ever produced on Planet Earth. Man's most intelligent act occurs when he hears the Word of God and decides to receive it at face value—believe it and follow it, doing what it says. The intelligent way is the scriptural way.

Intelligent Praying Is Scriptural Praying

The Bible is God's prayer manual. Someone has suggested you will find something about prayer on almost every page. The Word of God is filled with prayers, praying, exhortations to pray, results of prayer, and examples of prayerfulness and prayerlessness. The Old Testament heroes were men and women of prayer. The apostles believed in prayer, preached it and practiced it. Paul's epistles are inexhaustible on the subject. Most important, Jesus was a man of prayer. Finally, God originated it, ordained it, inspires it, hears it and answers it. The Bible way is the wise way, the knowledgeable way and the common sense way. Scriptural praying is intelligent praying.

If the Bible is the Word of God, which do you think I should learn about God from—the Koran, the Book of Mormon or the Bible? You can't learn to golf by reading a baseball manual. I would never teach my son to play football by having him watch Bo Jackson play baseball. We learn the ABCs of praying by reading God's book on prayer—the Bible. We learn how to pray by studying the men and women of God whose lives were examples of prayer. We also learn from the prayerfulness and prayerlessness of those around us. Intelligent praying has always been and will always be scriptural praying. The Bible tells us how to pray and how *not* to pray.

Prayer Practices We Should Avoid

One of the strongest how-to chapters in the Gospels is Matthew 6. It tells us how to give, how to fast, how to handle our money and how to be content. It also tells us how to pray. If you want to know how to do something, read the Word of God. The Bible will tell you. It is the authority. Scripture will instruct you. Not only does

Matthew 6 tell us how to pray, it also tells us how *not* to pray. Even the shades of meaning are illustrated in order that there be no misunderstanding. Let us consider some prayer practices we should avoid.

Avoid Praying As the Hypocrites
"And when thou prayest, thou shalt not be as the hypocrites are: for they love to pray standing in the synagogues and in the corners of the streets, that they may be seen of men. Verily I say unto you, They have their reward" (Matthew 6:5).

We cannot be as the hypocrites and expect answers to our prayers. A hypocrite is an insincere person, one who pretends to be what he is not. He acts out a false part and makes a false profession. He is a deceiver, a cheat, a pretender and an impostor. He seeks to cover up his real self in order to prosper by his deceit.

Jesus did not condemn standing while praying, praying in the synagogue or praying at street corners.

Jesus did condemn the vulgar ostentation of praying to be seen and heard of men. Standing was a frequent posture in prayer among the Jews of our Lord's day (Luke 18:11, 13). The same has been customary in many churches and among people on many continents in almost every era of Christendom. The issue was not the position but the spirit of show and display. Jesus said hypocrites take pleasure in searching out not only the largest, most pious gatherings but also the widest streets, busiest intersections and county courthouse squares so that they may "shine" and attract as much attention as possible. Their goal was to be "seen and heard of men." Their love was not of prayer nor of God but of being noticed and having men's applause. Their goal was not to be seen and heard of God but to attract the attention and acclaim of men.

Jesus said if this is what they want, then let them receive it because that is the only reward they will get. Praying as the hypocrites pray is a practice we should avoid.

Avoid Praying As the Heathen

"When ye pray, use not vain repetitions, as the heathen do: for they think that they shall be heard for their much speaking. Be not ye therefore like unto them: for your Father knoweth what things ye have need of, before ye ask him" (Matthew 6:7, 8). The two great faults Jesus mentioned here were vainglory (praying as the hypocrites) and vain repetitions (praying as the heathen).

Even though prayer is lifting up the soul and pouring out the heart, Christ warns us not to repeat empty phrases over and over again. The heathen supposed that by multiplying their prayers, their answers would also be multiplied. To repeat words without meaning is certainly vain repetition, like the prophets of Baal who cried all morning, "O Baal, hear us" (1 Kings 18:26). The Ephesian mob kept shouting for two hours, "Great is Diana of the Ephesians" (Acts 19:34). There was then, and still is today, a subconscious idea that if men batter long enough at God's door, He will answer, as if God can be talked, and even pestered, into agreement. So many confuse verbosity with piety and fluency with devotion. This is a mistake.

Jesus did not forbid "much praying" for He often spent whole nights in prayer. He did not forbid repeating the same words, phrases and thoughts in prayer, for He did this with much agony and intensity in the Garden of Gethsemane. But the belief that the number and the length of one's prayers are the determining factors in receiving an answer, that prayers will be heard not because they are the genuine desire of the heart but because of their length and the number of times they are repeated, is a false assump-

tion. There is a definite distinction between "much praying" and "much speaking." Christ was speaking of the
continual babbling about things which are irrelevant and
senseless. Praying to God is serious business. Heathenish
repetition is dangerous business. God wants us to say
what we mean and mean what we say from the bottom of
our heart. All of the words in the world are not equivalent
to one holy desire. Even the best-sounding prayers are
vain repetition if they are not the language of the heart.

"Your Father knoweth what things ye have need of,
before ye ask him," Jesus said. God is our Father! In prayer
we acknowledge Him, confess our need of Him and plead
our dependency upon Him. Children do not make long
speeches to their parents. They come to the point in as few
words as possible. We come to God not to inform Him but
to worship Him. Let us come to Him with the disposition
of children, with love, reverence and a trusting dependency, crying, "Abba, Father." He knows us and our situation better than we know ourselves. He knows the things
we have need of. "The eyes of the Lord run to and fro
throughout the whole earth, to shew himself strong in the
behalf of them whose heart is perfect toward him" (2
Chronicles 16:9). He often gives before we call (Isaiah
65:24) and is able to do even more for us than we can think
to ask (Ephesians 3:20).

Indeed, Helen and I have learned that our Father does
know our needs even before we ask Him. When we first
began our ministry, we packed our few belongings, bought
a bus ticket and headed for the ministers meeting in Weath-
erford, Texas. Booking our first revival in Port Arthur, we
caught a ride with District Overseer Henry (and his wife,
Millie) Ellis of Tyler. Pastor Esel Gibson met us in Tyler,
and we drove down to Port Arthur to begin a wonderful
revival meeting. Everything was going well, with one

exception. We had scheduled meetings all across the state of Texas but had no transportation.

One day while praying for the services, I asked myself, *I wonder if it would be all right for me to pray and ask God to help us to have some means of transportation to travel from one revival to another?* During the day I would see a nice automobile go by, and I would look at it and say, *Oh, no, that one is too nice. I could never get up enough nerve to ask God for something that good.* About that time an old rattletrap would come clunking by, and I would say, *Now, maybe I could get up enough nerve to ask the Lord to help us get something similar to that one.*

While trying to get up the courage to pray the prayer, God was already solving the problem. He had picked out the car, one far superior to anything I would have ever dreamed of owning. He knew the distances we were scheduled to travel and the size of the churches in which we were to minister. God had already negotiated the down payment and made arrangements for the monthly installments. The only thing left for us to do was to sign the papers and say, "Thank You, Jesus." It was probably the best car deal I have ever received in my life. "Your Father knoweth what things ye have need of, before ye ask him" (Matthew 6:8).

Praying as the hypocrites and the heathen is unintelligent praying. Praying with vain repetition and to be seen and heard of men is not very intelligent. *Lord, teach us to pray intelligently!*

Prayer Practices We Should Learn

In Matthew 6:5, 7, 8 Jesus teaches us about prayer practices we should avoid. These could easily be labeled "how *not* to pray." However, the Bible also tells us how *to* pray.

Following are a few basic lessons we need to learn about prayer.

Pray According to Christ's Model Prayer

"After this manner therefore pray ye: Our Father which art in heaven, Hallowed be thy name. Thy kingdom come. Thy will be done in earth, as it is in heaven. Give us this day our daily bread. And forgive us our debts, as we forgive our debtors. And lead us not into temptation, but deliver us from evil: For thine is the kingdom, and the power, and the glory, for ever. Amen" (Matthew 6:9-13).

Pray by Asking

James said, "Ye have not, because ye ask not" (4:2). Did I ever learn this lesson early in life! I grew up in Charlotte, North Carolina, in the home of my foster grandparents, Mr. and Mrs. Freeman. (My mother, Sarah Margaret, was given to the Freemans when she was a baby. Her father was an alcoholic, and her mother didn't have the money to buy milk to feed Sarah Margaret.) Every Saturday, Grandpa Freeman managed to find a way to get to town. We lived in an area called Smokey Hollow, so called because three railroad lines crisscrossed about a block from our house— the Seaboard, the Norfolk and the Southern. To get downtown we would generally walk the railroad tracks. My little 8-year-old legs just barely reached from one crosstie to another. I remember that Grandpa Freeman would always buy me a sack of candy just before time to go home. I had known all day that it was coming, so my anticipation was sky-high. As usual, he would take the top of the sack and twist it tightly, saying to me, "Now let's wait until we get home, and Granny Freeman will help it to last longer. Sure enough, Granny Freeman would take the candy sack and untwist it, saying, "Now, Sonny, take one piece now, and Granny will put it up here in the cabinet so it will last longer." She knew just how long my short legs were and how high I could jump, so she would place the candy slightly out of my reach. I learned early how to pull on Granny Freeman's apron strings. I learned what James 4:2 means: "Ye have not, because ye ask not." And there were times when I did *more* than ask. I had absolutely no qualms about begging and pleading a little also.

Intelligent praying is not built on the premise that if we just ignore a problem, it will go away. The Bible says in Matthew 7:8-11, "For every one that asketh receiveth; and he that seeketh findeth; and to him that knocketh it shall be opened. Or what man is there of you, whom if his son ask bread, will he give him a stone? Or if he ask a fish, will he give him a serpent? If ye then, being evil, know how to give good gifts unto your children, how much more shall your Father which is in heaven give good things to them that ask him?" Jesus' words in Matthew 6:8, "Your Father knoweth what things ye have need of, before ye ask him," mean that God expects us to *ask* Him.

What father is there who has never been asked? Jesus said in Matthew 18:19, "If two of you shall agree on earth as touching any thing that they shall ask, it shall be done for them of my Father which is in heaven." He also said, "And all things, whatsoever ye shall ask in prayer, believing, ye shall receive" (Matthew 21:22) and "If ye abide in me, and my words abide in you, ye shall ask what ye will, and it shall be done unto you" (John 15:7).

We need to learn to pray according to Christ's model prayer and to pray by asking.

Ask With Right Motives

James 4:3 cautions, "Ye ask, and receive not, because ye ask amiss, that ye may consume it upon your lusts." The

Living Bible says it like this: "The reason you don't have what you want is that you don't ask God for it. And even when you do ask you don't get it because your whole aim is wrong—you want only what will give *you* pleasure" (4:2, 3). If your motives are all wrong when you pray, nothing happens because you've missed the whole point and intent of prayer.

To lust is to desire and long for something. One who covets something could also desire the removal of the former possessor of that thing. James was saying the lustful, murdering, contentious person cannot pray properly. The Judaizers desired the conversion of the heathen, not for the glory of God and the salvation of the lost but to increase the amount of their coffers for their own self-indulgence. It was wrong then and it is wrong now. Lust for power, dominion, pleasure and riches causes wars, strife, envying and seditions. The ax needs to be laid to the root of the tree. We need to mortify the lusts and inordinate desires which struggle within. Such lust cancels out prayer. When our prayers are the language of our lusts, we disgrace devotion and dishonor God. It is treason to set the world upon the throne of our hearts. "And whatsoever we ask, we receive of him, because we keep his commandments, and do those things that are pleasing in His sight" (1 John 3:22).

Ask According to His Will

"And this is the confidence that we have in him, that, if we ask any thing according to his will, he heareth us: And if we know that He hear us, whatsoever we ask, we know that we have the petitions that we desired of him" (1 John 5:14, 15).

The story is told of a young man who was courting a young lady named Lillian. While talking with his pastor,

he mentioned he and Lillian were in love and were thinking about getting married. The pastor responded that
marriage was a very serious lifetime decision, that he should
consult with both their parents and make the whole thing a
matter of prayer. "Be sure to pray for God's will to be done
in both your lives." The young man thanked his pastor and
rushed home to pray, "O Lord, have Thy will, but give me
Lill."

A lot of people want God to have His will so long as His
will corresponds with their will. Asking according to
God's will is the same thing as asking according to God's
Word. Once again we go to the Scripture and to the
example of Jesus' prayer to His heavenly Father in the
Garden of Gethsemane: "Nevertheless not my will, but
thine, be done" (Luke 22:42). This is intelligent praying.

Ask in His Name

"And whatsoever ye shall ask in my name, that will I do,
that the Father may be glorified in the Son. If ye shall ask
any thing in my name, I will do it" (John 14:13, 14). "Ye
have not chosen me, but I have chosen you, and ordained
you, that ye should go and bring forth fruit, and that your
fruit should remain: that whatsoever ye shall ask of the
Father in my name, he may give it you" (15:16). "Verily,
verily I say unto you, Whatsoever ye shall ask the Father in
my name, he will give it you. . . . Ask, and ye shall receive,
that your joy may be full" (16:23, 24).

We have a High Priest and His name is Jesus. He can be
touched with "the feeling of our infirmities." He does
sympathize and identify with our vulnerability. He, too,
was tempted, tested and tried in every way, exactly as we
have been. And He did it without giving up or giving in.
Let us, therefore, by His open invitation, come boldly unto
His very throne with courage and confidence. Let us

continue coming in freedom and without hesitation, staying until we receive whatever help we must have for our times of need (Hebrews 4:14-16).

Jesus directed us to pray in His name. It is our key of access to the throne room of God. There is no other way to pray your prayer except by and through the name of Jesus. To pray in His name acknowledges Jesus as our Savior. To pray in His name acknowledges our sin. It also acknowledges the cross of Christ as God's remedy for sin. Jesus himself said "that whosoever believeth in him should not perish, but have everlasting life" (John 3:16).

Prayer

Thank You, Father, for teaching us how to pray and how not to pray. We receive Your Holy Word as our guide for life. Please forgive us for our misconceptions and preconceived ideas. Hear our prayer and receive our worship through Jesus Christ our Lord, we pray. Amen.

CHAPTER

—— 3 ——

PRAYING
DIRECTLY

It is said that people go to church on Sunday morning because the *pastor* is popular and go on Sunday evening because the *church* is popular. It is also said that people go to church on prayer meeting night because *God* is popular. I like to think everyone goes to church every time because God is popular. Psalm 122:1 says, "I was glad when they said unto me, Let us go into the house of the Lord." What a thrill it is to "enter into his gates with thanksgiving, and into his courts with praise" and what a privilege it is to "be thankful unto him, and bless his name" (Psalm 100:4).

Prayer is a wonderful ministry. Everyone should be involved as a prayer warrior in the ministry of intercessory prayer. From the earliest days of my life, I learned that I cannot function without prayer. My mother taught me to pray. My grandparents taught me to pray. My pastors, Sunday school teachers and many others have shown me the necessity of prayer. I cannot remember when I did not pray. How blessed I have been to be surrounded all of my life by those who pray. It happened in the churches I pastored, in the revivals we conducted, in youth camps, camp meetings and in overseas missionary crusades.

Whenever and wherever prayer was offered, it was always a vital and necessary part of my life.

I was conducting my first revival meeting at the Hemphill Avenue Church in Atlanta, Georgia, now the Mt. Paran congregation. I knew the task was too great for me alone. Impressed by the Holy Spirit, I visited the Sunday school classes, recruiting children, young people and adults to pray for the revival. One class I visited was the ladies Bible class. Sitting in the class was Sister Jeanie Wylie, former head matron of the girls orphanage. She had known me since I was a boy. Present also was Sister Lula Watson who had said to me many times, "Bennie Triplett, we are praying for you." Each evening as I stood trembling in that pulpit, I would look back over the congregation and see the prayer warriors assembled in my behalf. Suddenly I would feel 10 feet tall. I knew any sinner entering the building would be besieged with love, compassion and conviction that would never let go, give up or give in. Prayer is a wonderful ministry. I cannot function without the power of prayer in my life, for it is totally indispensable in the work of the Lord.

In Matthew 6:6 we read, "But thou, when thou prayest, enter into thy closet, and when thou hast shut thy door, *pray to the Father* which is in secret; and thy Father which seeth in secret shall reward thee openly." There are four points which I want to emphasize: first of all, go directly to the place of prayer; second, go directly to the source of prayer; third, get directly to the point of prayer; and finally, expect to receive a direct answer to your prayers.

Go Directly to the Place of Prayer
Going directly to the place of prayer could read, "Go directly to prayer." The Bible says, "When thou prayest, enter into thy closet" and shut the door. Everyone ought to

have a "spiritual closet" where they can enter for a time of prayer. The word *closet* has many meanings. It is from the Greek word *tameion* and can refer to a secret chamber, a small room, an inner court, a holy mountain, an upper room, a temple or a tabernacle. One commentator described the "closet" of Matthew 6:6 as a *sanctum*—a sacred place, a private room where a person can go and not be disturbed, a place set apart as a holy of holies, secure, serene or a special storehouse where only you and God have a key. The *place* of prayer is more spiritual and attitudinal than geographical and physical. The Bible speaks of *multiple* places of prayer such as the altar of sacrifice in Genesis 12:7, 8; 13:4; walking in an open field in Genesis 18:23-33; and standing by a well in Genesis 24:12-14. Some places of prayer even seem a bit *peculiar*, such as Jacob praying while wrestling in Genesis 32:24-30; Balaam praying while riding on a talking ass in Numbers 22:34; Samson praying while bound in chains to a mill in Judges 16:21-31; Job praying from an ash heap in Job 2:8, 3:1-26; and Jonah praying from the belly of a great fish in Jonah 2:1. The rich man prayed in hell and so did Jonah (Luke 16:19-31; Jonah 2:2). Jesus prayed while being baptized in the river Jordan (Luke 3:21, 22), in the wilderness (Luke 5:16), at the tomb of Lazarus (John 11:41, 42) and while hanging on the cross dying for our sins (Luke 23:34). Paul and Silas prayed in the Philippian jail (Acts 16:25) and during a shipwreck (Acts 27:23-35). The final place I will mention refers to the souls under the altar crying, "How long, O Lord, how long?" (Revelation 6:9-11).

Just as Jesus prayed at a certain place (Luke 11:1), God wants us to enter that certain place of sanctity whereby we can walk softly before Him. We take off our shoes as did Moses, because the ground on which we stand is holy ground (Exodus 3:5). Jesus said when you pray, enter into your closet and shut the door. It is as though the whole earth is the temple of God, and man can enter a secret invisible chamber anytime, anyplace, shutting out the whole world and shutting in the God of the universe. Could it be that the heart of man is the closet to which one can retire and converse with God and God alone? Could it be that the soul of man is that inner sanctum to which one can flee and shut the door in the face of all doubt, difficulties, negativism and opposition? Go directly to the place of prayer, and abandon yourself totally to the God of prayer and shut your door. The shutting of the door often has a double effect. It shuts some things out and refuses to let them in. It also shuts other things in and refuses to let them out. Slam the door on fear and open the door to faith. Close the entry way to despair and open your life to hope. Shut out the darkness, and let the light shine in. Bar the sanctuary of your soul to evil and make forever welcome the presence of good. Rather than standing in synagogues and on street corners to be seen and heard of men, Jesus expects His followers to seek out a designated and inconspicuous "closet" with a limited amount of space and a door to control any intrusions from the outside. *Lord, teach us to pray directly.*

Go Directly to the Source of Prayer

Jesus said very emphatically, "Pray to thy Father."

Prayer Is a Divine Arrangement

It is a power and a privilege which brings Divinity and humanity together. Jesus used the second person singular (you) for emphasis and contrast in Matthew 6:6: "But thou [you], when thou [you] prayest . . . pray to thy [your] Father." How we need to recognize the *source* of our strength and blessings! David said, "I will lift up mine eyes unto the hills, from whence cometh my help. My help cometh from the Lord, which made heaven and earth" (Psalm 121:1, 2). "Unto thee lift I up mine eyes, O thou that dwellest in the heavens" (Psalm 123:1).

The most heartfelt longing of any human being is for living communion with God himself. "As the hart (deer) panteth after the water brooks, so panteth my soul after thee, O God. My soul thirsteth for God, for the living God: when shall I come and appear before God?" (Psalm 42:1, 2). "O God, thou art my God; early will I seek thee: my soul thirsteth for thee, my flesh longeth for thee in a dry and thirsty land, where no water is" (Psalm 63:1). "My soul longeth, yea, even fainteth for the courts of the Lord: my heart and my flesh crieth out for the living God" (Psalm 84:2).

God has everything to do with prayer, and prayer has everything to do with God. The first great principle of prayer is God. That is why Jesus taught His disciples in Matthew 6:9, 10, "After this manner therefore pray ye: Our Father which art in heaven, Hallowed be thy name. Thy kingdom come. Thy will be done in earth, as it is in heaven." Prayer describes those rare and precious moments when man escapes the mundane, gets away from the ordinary and gets alone with God. Man spends far too much of his time with other things and other people. He spends far too little time with his Creator and Sustainer. God receives so little of our time and ourselves. In Genesis 24:63, Isaac went out into the field to meditate and be alone with God. Jesus often went into the mountains to pray and sometimes would spend the night in solitude with His heavenly Father (Luke 6:12). Peter went upon the housetop to pray in Acts 10:9 to avoid distraction and clear his mind for the voice of God.

Two Great Rules of Prayer

First, all true prayer must be offered to God. The Pharisees prayed to men, not to God. As William Barclay quotes, "After an ornate and elaborate prayer was offered in the Boston church, a great preacher remarked, 'That was the most eloquent prayer ever offered to a Boston audience.' " The person praying was more concerned with impressing the people than he was with making contact with his Maker. Whether in public prayer or private prayer, a man should have no thought in his mind and no desire in his heart but God. Secret prayer is one of the surest indicators of true piety and spirituality. Pray to God, and let that be enough.

Second, the God to whom we pray is Father of all. Jesus said, "Pray to thy Father" (Matthew 6:6) and "your Father knoweth what things ye have need of, before ye ask him" (Matthew 6:8). The divine arrangement of prayer cannot possibly be improved upon. Look at the directness of approach. "But thou, when thou prayest, enter into thy closet, and when thou hast shut thy door." Look at the directness of application and relationship. "Pray to thy Father." We are to pray to our Father who is love, who cares, who is present, who listens, hears and understands. Pray to Him as Father, one who is more ready and willing to answer prayer than we are ready and willing to pray. Pray to Him as one who is especially near and graciously inclined to help and sustain us. The whole philosophy of prayer is that we acknowledge Him as Father and ask for something as a child would ask his parent.

Romans 8:15 and Galatians 4:6 declare that we are not slaves, but children, by adoption and therefore we cry, "Abba, Father." Who is this God to whom we pray? He is our heavenly Father! We are His sons and daughters by adoption and by the miracle of the new birth. "But as many as received him, to them gave he power to become the sons of God, even to them that believe on his name" (John 1:12). A believer's prayer is a child's petition to an omniscient, omnipresent, omnipotent Father God. It is an unshakable, immutable relationship which shatters the uniformity of all other laws and arrangements.

Why Some Experiment With Other Than God's Arrangement

Like Pharaoh, some doubt the existence of God and His ability to answer prayer. "And Pharaoh said, Who is the Lord, that I should obey his voice to let Israel go? I know not the Lord, neither will I let Israel go" (Exodus 5:2). Isaiah 59:1 counters, "Behold, the Lord's hand is not shortened, that it cannot save; neither his ear heavy, that it cannot hear."

Some pray to idols and images made by the hands of man. "And God spake all these words saying....Thou shalt have no other gods before me. Thou shalt not make unto thee any graven image, or any likeness of any thing that is in heaven above, or that is in the earth beneath, or that is in the water under the earth. Thou shalt not bow down thyself to them, nor serve them: for I the Lord thy God am a jealous God" (Exodus 20:1, 3-5).

Some pray to the fantasies created by the imaginations of men. "The idols of the heathen are silver and gold, the works of men's hands. They have mouths, but they speak not; eyes have they, but they see not; they have ears, but they hear not; neither is there any breath in their mouths. They that make them are like unto them; so is everyone that trusteth in them" (Psalm 135:15-18).

As then, even now some worship and put their trust in the sun, moon and stars, rather than the one who created them, regulates them and sustains them.

Still others worship the creature more than the creator. They put their trust in human institutions and man-made philosophies. When man leaves the true God in order to serve and to give his allegiance to any false god, it is spoken of in the Scriptures as whoredom (Exodus 34:15, 16). Go to the Father who loves you and has provided everything you need—there is no need to go anywhere else.

Get Directly to the Point

Once we are in our special place of prayer, talking directly with our Father, that special person of prayer, there is really no need to beat around the bush. Why not get directly to the point of our prayer? "Pray to thy Father which is in secret" (Matthew 6:6). Oh, the universal presence of God who is in all secret places, who is where no one else is and is especially near when we call Him! Why, then, would we hold back? Does He not know the end from the beginning and the beginning from the end? Is He not omniscient—knowing all things? Does He not know what things we need even before we ask Him? Then why do we tease Him and play games with Him? The whole idea of holding back is totally out of character.

Did you ever have someone say to you, "Friend, I have a very special problem I would like to share if we could get together for a brief chat." And you say, "Why yes, let's get together tomorrow for a cup of coffee." Then the next day during coffee the conversation rambles on and on through World War I, II, and who knows what else. The individual has yet to get to the point and to the problem. Suddenly you realize that is the problem. There is a counselor who can set the counselee at ease. It is Jesus—our advocate, our go-between, our intercessor—Jesus, whom Isaiah called "Wonderful, Counsellor, The mighty God, The everlasting Father, The Prince of Peace" (Isaiah 9:6).

If you will observe the characters of the Book, it certainly did not take them long to get directly to the point. A leper said to Jesus, "Lord, if thou wilt, thou canst make me clean. And Jesus put forth his hand, and touched him, saying, I will; be thou clean. And immediately his leprosy was cleansed" (Matthew 8:2, 3). Not only did the leper get to the point, so did Jesus! Likewise, the woman with the issue of blood expended her last bit of strength to lunge through the flowing crowd in order to touch the hem of His tunic, saying in her heart, "If I may but touch his garment, I shall be whole." The Bible said that Jesus turned in His tracks and seeing her said, "Daughter, be of good comfort; thy faith hath made thee whole. And the woman was made whole from that hour" (Matthew 9:20-22).

Getting to the point is another way of saying, "Yes, Lord, I believe." Beating around the bush says, "I'm not sure. Maybe You will, and maybe You won't. Maybe You should, and maybe You shouldn't." Did He not suggest that we enter our closet and shut the door—shutting out all artificiality, all superfluity, all protocol and red tape, all pretense and self-aggrandizement? He wants us to take the mask off and meet Him face-to-face at the foot of the Cross where the ground is level for all men and women.

It reminds me somewhat of the Pharisee and the publican in Luke 18:10-14. The Pharisee began his prayer with a long preamble, setting the stage for an elaborate oration, cataloging his credentials and listing his references. His main theme was, "I thank thee that I am not as other men are" (v. 11). The publican, however, stood some distance away and would not even lift up his eyes unto heaven, but rather smote his breast and said, "God be merciful to me a sinner" (v. 13). Jesus said in verse 14, "I tell you, this man went down to his house justified rather than the other: for every one that exalteth himself shall be abased; and he that humbleth himself shall be exalted."

Hebrews 4:16 advises, "Let us therefore come boldly

unto the throne of grace, that we may obtain mercy, and find grace to help in time of need."

Expect to Receive a Direct Answer

Establish directly the place of prayer. Go directly to the source of prayer. Get directly to the point of prayer, and expect to receive a direct answer to your prayer. The last phrase of Matthew 6:18 reassures, "And thy Father, which seeth in secret, shall reward thee openly." Already you are noticing the contrasts found in this verse with other verses, such as those who pray openly and receive no reward versus those who pray secretly and are rewarded openly. Since this point seems to be the bottom line on *direct praying*, I want us to take a close look at the total meaning of this special phrase.

First of all, God hears us. "And this is the confidence that we have in him, that, if we ask any thing according to his will, he heareth us: And if we know that he hear us, whatsoever we ask, we know that we have the petitions that we desired of Him" (1 John 5:14, 15). "The Lord is far from the wicked: but he heareth the prayer of the righteous" (Proverbs 15:29). "And *Samuel* cried unto the Lord for Israel; and the Lord heard him" (1 Samuel 7:9). *David* said, "I sought the Lord, and he heard me, and delivered me from all my fears" (Psalm 34:4). "I cried by reason of mine affliction unto the Lord, and he heard me; out of the belly of hell cried I, and thou heardest my voice" (Jonah 2:2). "But the angel said unto him, Fear not, Zacharias: for thy prayer is heard; and thy wife Elizabeth shall bear thee a son, and thou shalt call his name John" (Luke 1:13). In Acts 10:31 the angel said to Cornelius, "Thy prayer is heard."

Second, God not only hears us—He sees us. Jesus seems to enjoy pointing out the details of His Father's loving care for His children. The word He uses refers to both bodily vision and mental perception. It means not only to look by the use of the eyes with the power to see, it means also to discern, discover and understand by the use of the mind's eye and a sense of feeling as well as seeing. To say that God reads each of us like an open book is an understatement. God is omniscient. He not only knows all things, He sees all things. Did He not say to Satan, "Hast thou considered my servant, Job?" (Job 1:8). God had considered him. He knew Job like the back of His hand. He had thoroughly considered Job, weighing him, examining him and evaluating his commitment. He had tried him by fire and found him to be pure gold (Zechariah 13:9; Job 23:10). What a commendation and recommendation! How many of us can pray:

> Search me, O God, and know my heart today;
> Try me, O Savior, know my thoughts I pray:
> See if there be some wicked way in me:
> Cleanse me from ev'ry sin, and set me free.
> —J. Edwin Orr

God sees us openly, and He sees us secretly. Did He not say to Nathanael in John 1:48, "When thou wast under the fig tree, I saw thee"? Did He not say to Ananias in Acts 9:11, "Arise, and go into the street which is called Straight, and enquire in the house of Judas for one called Saul, of Tarsus: for, behold, he prayeth"? God not only hears our prayers, He also sees the one who is praying. God knows our temporary or permanent address. He knows what street we live on and the house we reside in. When the eye of no one is upon you to applaud you, His eye is upon you to accept you and to aid you. God hears us. God sees us.

God is always glad to welcome us. The story is told of a young lad whose father was a prominent business executive with an office on the top floor of a downtown skyscraper.

The son loved his father, and the father loved his son. The lad had never had the opportunity to visit his father's office complex. One day on returning home from school, he felt he must talk with his dad. He could not wait for his father's arrival from the office, so, on his own, he walked downtown, went into the office complex and pushed the top button of the elevator. Arriving on the top floor, the lad proceeded through the large glass doors with his father's name etched on the company's insignia. Marching down the main aisle, he continued toward the large mahogany doors. Numerous secretaries and vice presidents tried in vain to get his attention or stop him on his quest. Reaching the main office, the small boy twisted the brass knob and was suddenly standing before the president. Much to the relief of all the staff out front, they heard these words, "Good evening, son. Your father is very proud to see you! Now, what can I do for you today?"

Third, God hears, sees and answers prayer. Elijah prayed directly to God and received a direct answer. He prayed for a drought and received a three-and-a-half-year dry spell (James 5:17). Again he prayed for fire and the Bible said, "The fire of the Lord fell, and consumed the burnt sacrifice, and the wood, and the stones, and the dust, and licked up the water that was in the trench. And when all the people saw it, they fell on their faces: and they said, The Lord, He is the God: The Lord, He is the God" (1 Kings 18:36-39).

God rewards us openly. Answers to our prayers and rewards to our petitions fit into a special category. Jesus said we would not lose our reward. Ours will be one of grace and not one of debt. Answers from God come from an abundant storehouse where there is no lack of supply. As the chorus explains, "Every promise in the book is mine, every chapter, every verse, every line."

Prayers are rewarded openly. Even secret prayers have

a hard time hiding open answers. "He that heareth and seeth in secret shall reward thee openly" (Matthew 6:6).

How, may I ask, will you hide the joy of sins forgiven? How can you contain rivers of living water spoken of in John 7:38? How are we going to stamp "top secret" on Malachi 3:10 which says, "Prove me now herewith, said the Lord of hosts, if I will not open to you the windows of heaven, and pour you out a blessing, that there shall not be room enough to receive it." Openly means generously, manifestly, publicly, graciously and honorably. Friend, that is about as direct as one can be.

When Helen and I were assigned to North and South Dakota as overseer, we knew that both states were considered home missionary territory. A quick study of its history revealed that most of the congregations had been started in small villages and rural areas. As a result more congregations had been disbanded than had survived. The reason was very simple. For the most part the cities and population centers had been bypassed. Upon our arrival, a prime unfinished project was to establish a church in Grand Forks—North Dakota's second largest city. The report was "all odds are against you, no property, no building, no finance . . . only committed and dedicated workers."

I took the news of the project to all the churches and asked the people to help us pray. "Please help us to pray," I asked, "that the walls of Jericho will fall flat." A strange request indeed! We needed all opposition to cease and for God to do what He wanted to do. We had no idea how God was going to answer our prayer. We simply kept praying and believing. Much to our surprise a strong, prestigious congregation began fellowshipping with our people. Then one day they requested the privilege of uniting with our church. Today one of our strongest congregations stands in that university city of North Dakota—a bulwark of faith *and* a definite answer to prayer.

CHAPTER

4

PRAYING
EXPECTANTLY

Expect great things, attempt great things, and you will experience great things. The dream, the hope and the vision always precedes the reality. "Where there is no vision, the people perish" (Proverbs 29:18). "Your young men shall see visions, and your old men shall dream dreams" (Acts 2:17). Every new and succeeding generation must continue to dream the impossible dream and to visualize the possible vision. "Now faith is the substance (or the reality) of things hoped for, the evidence (or the proof) of things not seen" (Hebrews 11:1).

What do we mean by praying *expectantly*? Let us consider the following four points: expect God to do *what* He said He would do; expect God to do it *when* He said He would do it; expect God to do it *where* and *as* He has promised; expect God to do it to *whom* He said it. "And Jesus answering saith unto them, Have faith in God. For verily I say unto you, That whosoever shall say unto this mountain, Be thou removed, and be thou cast into the sea; and shall not doubt in his heart, but shall believe that those things which he saith shall come to pass; he shall have whatsoever he saith. Therefore I say unto you, What things soever ye desire, when ye pray, believe that ye receive them, and ye shall have them" (Mark 11:22-24)." My soul, wait thou only upon God; for my expectation is from him" (Psalm 62:5).

What We Mean by the Word *Expect*

In the Scriptures the English word *expect* has two forms in the original Greek. The first is the compound word *ekdechomai*, made up of a prepositional prefix *ek* meaning "from" or "out of," and the word *dechomai*, which means "to receive, to wait, to receive from, or to wait for something from someone." It is a reaching out of one's total being in readiness to receive. It is looking for, waiting for, tarrying for and watching for something from someone. This kind of anticipation is found throughout the Word of God.

A second New Testament word is *apokaradokia*. It is a triple word made up of *apo*, which means "from"; *kara*, which means "the head"; and *dokia*, which means "to watch with an outstretched head." My first encounter with this concept was one of mild confusion. I had always been accustomed to waiting to receive with an outstretched *hand*. According to the meaning in the original language, God has chosen by His wisdom to teach us to *expect* by watching with an outstretched *head*. It speaks of a strained expectancy, an eager longing for something from a certain place or a certain person.

Abstraction

The prepositional prefix *apo* meaning "from" has double action. One is negative and the other is positive. The negative is called an abstraction. The positive is called absorption. Abstraction means anything that engages our minds, attracts our attention and keeps us away from the anticipation of expectation. Abstraction subtracts, takes away from, draws away and separates by a mental absentmindedness. Satan is a genius in mind control. It probably started in the Garden of Eden. The Scriptures warn us and constantly call for self-discipline in this regard.

"Let us lay aside every weight, and the sin which doth so easily beset us, and let us run with patience the race that is set before us, looking unto Jesus the author and finisher of our faith" (Hebrews 12:1, 2).

"Wherefore lay apart all filthiness and superfluity of naughtiness, and receive with meekness the engrafted word, which is able to save your souls" (James 1:21).

Abstraction is the opposite of absorption. Abstraction keeps us away from the anxious longing of expectation and causes us to lose our desire for the things God has promised.

A friend used to tell how, when he was growing up, his mom required him to practice the piano on certain days. Every day that he was supposed to stay in and practice, his buddies in the community would gang up outside and have a football game. Can't you just see a young man trying to practice the piano while all his buddies are outside playing football? He said the only way he was able to do it was with the help of a "persuader," which his mother used to make sure he was not distracted. "In fact," he said, "Mom's *persuader* turned out to be more powerful than the scheme my buddies had hatched up to keep me from doing the things I was supposed to be doing." He became a great pianist and a good football player.

Absorption

Not only is there a negative part, there is also a positive. There is a distraction, and there is an attraction. There is an abstraction, and there is an absorption. Absorption means being fully caught up in the object that is expected until the fulfillment is totally realized.

"And unto them that look for him shall he appear the second time without sin unto salvation" (Hebrews 9:28).

"If ye then be risen with Christ, seek those things which are above, where Christ sitteth on the right hand of God. Set your *affections* on things above, not on things on the earth" (Colossians 3:1, 2).

"But seek ye first the kingdom of God, and his righteousness; and all these things shall be added unto you" (Matthew 6:33).

One Mind, One Accord

Those in the Upper Room who received the outpouring of the Pentecostal blessing were in one mind, one accord and in one place. They had one desire, one goal and one ambition—to be clothed with the power of God from on high, which they had been promised. One of the secrets of the victory and triumph the early church enjoyed was to be deliberately absorbed in God's promise, refusing to be distracted.

When we approach God in prayer, our minds need to be turned totally toward Him in a sense of longing and anticipation. How we need to live and breathe the things of God! He wants us to become engrossed in Him, His work and His Word. He wants us to "taste and see that the Lord is good" (Psalm 34:8). He wants us to be attracted, not distracted.

Expect God to Do What He Said He Would Do
Salvation

Do you want to be saved? "That if thou shalt confess with thy mouth the Lord Jesus, and shalt believe in thine heart that God hath raised him from the dead, thou shalt be saved" (Romans 10:9). Don't doubt it. Expect it!

Sanctification

Do you want to be sanctified? "Wherefore Jesus also, that he might sanctify the people with his own blood, suffered without the gate" (Hebrews 13:12). "We are sanctified through the offering of the body of Jesus Christ once for all" (Hebrews 10:10). Don't doubt it. Expect it!

Filled With the Spirit

Do you want to be filled with the Spirit? "And be not drunk with wine, wherein is excess; but be filled with the Spirit; speaking to yourselves in psalms and hymns and spiritual songs, singing and making melody in your heart to the Lord" (Ephesians 5:18, 19).

"That we might receive the promise of the Spirit through faith" (Galatians 3:14).

"And when they had prayed, the place was shaken where they were assembled together; and they were all filled with the Holy Ghost, and they spake the word of God with boldness" (Acts 4:31).

"For the promise is unto you, and to your children, and to all that are afar off, even as many as the Lord our God shall call" (Acts 2:39).

Don't doubt it. Expect it!

Healed

Do you want to be healed?

"He sent his word and healed them, and delivered them from their destructions" (Psalm 107:20).

"And with his stripes we are healed" (Isaiah 53:5). "And the power of the Lord was present to heal them" (Luke 5:17).

"Is there any sick among you? let him call for the elders of the church; and let them pray over him, anointing him with oil in the name of the Lord: and the prayer of faith shall save the sick, and the Lord shall raise him up" (James 5:14, 15).

Don't doubt it. Expect it!

Blessings From God

Do you want to receive blessings from God? "Prove me now herewith, saith the Lord of hosts, if I will not open you the windows of heaven, and pour you out a blessing, that there shall not be room enough to receive it" (Malachi 3:10). "Call unto me, and I will answer thee, and show thee great and mighty things, which thou knowest not" (Jeremiah 33:3). Don't doubt it. Expect it!

Lord, teach us to pray expectantly. Teach us to expect God to do what He promised He would do.

Expect God to Do It *When* He Promised He Would Do It

The wise man of the Old Testament says, "There is a *time* for every thing" (Ecclesiastes 3:1, *NIV*). Verse 11 says, "He has made everything beautiful in its time." God not only has a *what* that He can do, but He also has a *when* He wants to do it.

There Is a Time for All Things

"In due time Christ died" (Romans 5:6). There was a time for the death of Jesus Christ, and there was a time for His resurrection. There was a time for the ascension of our Lord and the beginning of His mediatorial ministry. "The time is at hand" (Revelation 22:10). God has a time that we can expect things from Him.

God Is Always on Time

"And it shall come to pass, that before they call, I will answer; and while they are yet speaking, I will hear" (Isaiah 65:24). Praise God, He is always on time. He has a system that we can depend on. Throughout the Word of God we see the chronological workings of an Almighty God. We can see the evidence of His hand, feel His immaculate touch, and sense His providential meaning coming forth as He puts it all together into a wonderful crescendo and a beautiful finale.

Expect God to Do It *Where* and As He Has Promised

We should not only expect *what* God has promised, *when* He has promised it, but should expect Him to do it *where* and *as* He desires to do so. In Acts 2:1 we read, "And when the day of Pentecost was fully come, they were all with one accord in one place." God has a *where* to perform His will, His wish and His design. The Bible says, "There came a sound from heaven as of a rushing mighty wind and it filled all the house *where* they were sitting" (Acts 2:2). The miracle goes on and on. The intricate details of His master plan are past finding out (Romans 11:33).

When the apostle Paul was going to Rome, a storm was encountered (Acts 27:20-25). Things were being thrown overboard, and everyone was in a state of panic. Paul went to the captain of the ship and asked for everyone's attention. He said to them, "Wherefore, sirs, be of good cheer: for there stood by me this night an angel of God, whose I am and whom I serve, saying, fear not, Paul; there shall not be any loss of life, but we will lose the ship." He said, "Everyone is going to be saved. Therefore, I believe God, and I expect that it will be even as it was told me."

Praise His Name! What God promises, He performs. Not only does He fulfill it *when* He promises, but if He indicates *where*, you can depend on that also. If He indicates every *i* will be dotted, and every *t* will be crossed, not one detail nor diacritical marking will be ignored. "One jot or one tittle shall in no wise pass from the law, till all be fulfilled" (Matthew 5:18).

God's Word is a contract agreement with your name at

the top and His name at the bottom. The cliché, "God said it, I believe it, and that settles it," has been called into question lately by someone suggesting, "God said it, and *that* settles it, whether we believe it or not."

I'm glad, however, that He allows us to believe. He wants us to believe, and He expects us to believe. How wonderful that He gives us the intelligence to read it, to understand it and to want to know about it.

C.S. Grogan puts it like this:

Tell me more, tell me more,
Tell me more about Jesus,
Never has a sweeter story been told.
Tell me more, tell me more,
Tell me more about Jesus.
Ever new, this story never grows old.

"But when he [the Prodigal Son] was yet a great way off, his father saw him, and had compassion, and ran, and fell on his neck, and kissed him" (Luke 15:20).

Expectancy—watching with an outstretched head and an outstretched heart; a strained expectancy, eager longing, looking, watching, tarrying, waiting and believing. Can you imagine the days, the hours, the weeks and the months that this silver-haired dad had turned his eyes in the direction his son had departed to become a prodigal? Do you have any idea of the wild imaginations which went through that father's mind and heart, not hearing from his boy, wondering what had happened to him?

For some reason, he never gave up. He never stopped hoping, praying, believing and expecting. Those eyes were getting feeble, the cataracts were beginning to form, and possibly he was having a hard time focusing. Probably, with the power of the mind, every now and then he would see a mirage that would appear as if something was darting from behind one bush and across to the other tree. With a watchful head, a watchful mind and an expectant heart, he longed for his son.

He never ceased believing the answer was on its way. It was going to happen. It was going to be fulfilled. His prayer would be answered.

You better believe there was a lot going on. There were times when those around him would say, "He's grieving himself to death. Why doesn't he forget that boy and enjoy what he has?" So there was always that abstraction and distraction trying to get him away. But because of his love, his hope and his faith, he became totally absorbed in the object of his faith. He refused to give up. "When he was a great way off, his father saw him, and had compassion, and ran and fell on his neck, and kissed him" (Luke 15:20).

Expect God to Do What He Said to *Whom* He Said It

Not only can we expect God to do *what* He said, *when* He said it and *where* He said it, but also to *whom* He said it. Listen to the call of His Word, through the voice of the Holy Spirit.

"If *my people*, which are called by my name, shall humble themselves, and pray, and seek my face, and turn from their wicked ways; then will I hear from heaven, and will forgive their sin, and will heal their land" (2 Chronicles 7:14).

"For God so loved the world, that he gave his only begotten Son, that *whosoever* believeth in him should not perish, but have everlasting life" (John 3:16).

"Come unto me, *all ye* that labour and are heavy laden, and I will give you rest. Take my yoke upon you, and learn of me; for I am meek and lowly in heart: and ye shall find rest unto your souls. For my yoke is easy, and my burden is light" (Matthew 11:28-30).

"If *we* confess *our* sins, he is faithful and just to forgive us our sins, and to cleanse us from all unrighteousness" (1 John 1:9).

That's the way faith works. It's a personal thing. "Faith is the *substance* of things hoped for, the *evidence* of things not seen" (Hebrews 11:1). The original suggests, "Faith is the reality of things being hoped for, the proof of things not having been seen." Just as prayer is personal, the results are also personal. God wants *you* to pray, to believe and to receive. Do it now! In Jesus' name, Amen.

CHAPTER

———5———

PRAYING
UNITEDLY

The Scriptures are replete with the concept of unity. Think of it—one mind, one place, one accord, one heart, one spirit, one soul, one purpose and one ambition. It is vital for all of us to be united in the things which we do. Of course, the opposite of being united is to be divided. The Bible speaks of a divided heart. "Every kingdom divided against itself is brought to desolation; and every city or house divided against itself shall not stand" (Matthew 12:25).

While God abhors disunity, He praises unity. "Teach me thy way, O Lord; I will walk in thy truth: unite my heart to fear thy name" (Psalm 86:11). "Behold, how good and how pleasant it is for brethren to dwell together in unity" (Psalm 133:1). "Endeavouring to keep the unity of the Spirit in the bond of peace" (Ephesians 4:3). "Till we all come in the unity of the faith, and of the knowledge of the Son of God, unto a perfect man, unto the measure of the stature of the fullness of Christ" (Ephesians 4:13). Anything done in a united way is usually accomplished in the most effective way. This is, by far, the best way to carry out all of the mandates of our Lord Jesus Christ.

It is also the best way to pray. "These all continued with one accord in prayer and supplication, with the women, and Mary the mother of Jesus, and with his brethren" (Acts 1:14). "And when the day of Pentecost was fully come they were all with one accord in one place" (Acts 2:1). The word *one*, as expressed in one mind, one accord and one place, is expressed two ways in the Scriptures. First, it is used as "one" in contrast to the "many."

> *Wherefore, as by one man sin entered into the world, and death by sin; and so death passed upon all men, for that all have sinned. . . . For if through the offence of one many be dead, much more the grace of God, and the gift by grace, which is by one man, Jesus Christ, hath abounded unto many. And not as it was by one that sinned, so is the gift: for the judgment was by one to condemnation, but the free gift is of many offenses unto justification. For if by one man's offence death reigned by one; much more they which receive abundance of grace and of the gift of righteousness shall reign in life by one, Jesus Christ. . . . For as by one man's disobedience many were made sinners, so by the obedience of one shall many be made righteous* (Romans 5:12, 15-17, 19).

A second meaning of the word *one* is its use as "one" to the exclusion of all others, such as "one and only one." "There is one body, and one Spirit, even as ye are called in one hope of your calling; one Lord, one faith, one baptism, One God and Father of all, who is above all, and through all, and in you all" (Ephesians 4:4-6).

This passage means *one* to the exclusion of all others. The one body is the church, the body of Christ. The one Spirit is the Holy Spirit. The one hope is the Christian's calling which is the one and only hope. The one Lord is the Lord Jesus Christ. The one faith is the gospel of the Lord Jesus Christ. The one baptism is the baptism of regeneration (Romans 6:3-7; 1 Corinthians 12:13; Galatians 3:27; Colossians 2:12). The one God is for all men, the Father of all. We do not need a God for the Jews, one for the Gentiles and another for whatever new group man might invent. We believe in one God eternally existing as Father of all.

The term *one accord* is from the compound Greek word *homo thumador* which means one mind, of the same thought and concept. It is synonymous with *togetherness*. We are not divided, we are one—in contrast to the many and to the exclusion of all others. We are one and only one united in the Lord Jesus Christ. A united prayer life produces the following results: prayer unites us in one place; prayer unites us in purpose; prayer unites us in spirit; prayer unites us with Jesus Christ.

Prayer Unites Us in One Place

"For where two or three are gathered together in my name, there am I in the midst of them" (Matthew 18:20).

Unity of One Place

This points out the simplicity of Christian worship in local churches. Christ's complete discourse points out the power of unity. "If two of you shall agree on earth as touching any thing that they shall ask, it shall be done for them of my Father which is in heaven" (Matthew 18:19). This talks about the coming together of our minds, and verse 20 speaks of the coming together of ourselves. "When this happens," Jesus says, "look for me! I'll be there!" The unity of believers assures the presence of Jesus. It's the kind of atmosphere He prefers. It's the kind of harmony He deserves.

The presence of Jesus is promised to a united worshiping body in one mind, in one accord and in one place. He is in tune with our harmony, and He is in agreement with our union. Prayer corrals the wild stallions of our minds and brings us together around the place of His presence. Supplication and intercession demand the roundup of our total being so that the whole Body can rally around Jesus Christ. "When this happens," Jesus interjects, "there I am in the midst." He is the apex as well as the center of every place of united prayer.

It is all too common to hear these words, "I do not need to go to church. The place is not important. Anyhow, this is the 20th century. I'll stay at home and watch television and listen to the radio. I'll read my Bible here and send my spirit to church." One pastor cautioned his congregation, "Don't send your spirit to church. Your spirit can't say 'Amen' to my preaching or give to the missionaries when the offering plate is passed."

The Bible warns us not to neglect "the assembling of ourselves together, as the manner of some is; but exhorting one another: and so much the more, as ye see the day approaching" (Hebrews 10:25). "These be they who separate themselves, sensual, having not the Spirit. But ye, beloved, building up yourselves on your most holy faith, praying in the Holy Ghost" (Jude 19, 20). "Praying always with all prayer and supplication in the Spirit, and watching thereunto with all perseverance and supplication for all saints" (Ephesians 6:18).

The Unity of a Few in One Place

Matthew 18:15-17 illustrates the power of a few in one place. Jesus pointed out that two can be used to counsel an individual or to condemn him in a trial. In some cases it may have serious consequences. The Scriptures are emphatic: two can move God through the power of prayer, and the needs of many can be supplied. Two believers constitute a local congregation which deserves and receives the very presence of Jesus—He is in their midst! They are His. They bear His insignia. They are gathered in His name to praise Him and invoke His power of attorney. Their place will be His place, and His place will be their place. Modern times and the present world crises demand unity. The church of the last days will survive only in unity.

Prayer Unites Us in Purpose

Prayer not only draws us together in one place, it also unites us in purpose.

Unity of Purpose

"If two of you shall agree . . . it shall be" (Matthew 18:19). Prayer brings us together. It harmonizes our wills to the will of God. As Jesus prayed in the Garden of Gethsemane, "Nevertheless not my will, but thine, be done" (Luke 22:42). In His model prayer for the disciples, Jesus taught them to pray, "Thy will be done in earth, as it is in heaven" (Matthew 6:10). Prayer brings heaven and earth together. The estrangement of the whole human race from the good graces of Jehovah God is because of the fall. Adam and Eve, by transgression, fell in the Garden of Eden. And the family of man has been out of sorts ever since. The inhabitants of the whole planet have gone AWOL. God has sent His Son, Jesus, to bring the earth back into a right relationship with God. Part of the heavenly strategy is the power of prayer, "Thy will be done in earth, as it is in heaven."

In Acts 15:23-29 we find a problem in one of the New Testament churches over the controversy of circumcision. Rather than being united, the congregation in Antioch had become divided. Some were saying, "The rest of you are not Christians because you are not doing what we think you ought to be doing." Their leaders sent to Jerusalem, to headquarters, to ask for an edict or a solution to their problem. Headquarters agreed unanimously to send a committee down to deal with the controversy. When the men returned to Jerusalem to report their results, there was such a spirit of unity and purpose that those who recorded the minutes of the meeting wrote, "For it seemed good to the Holy Ghost, and to us, to lay upon you no greater burden than these necessary things" (Acts 15:28). Prayer not only brings the will of God into our hearts, heaven to earth and the earth to heaven, but it unites our spirit with the Spirit of God.

What a difference the strategy of God can make in the solution of any problem. Before there was division and strife; now there is union and concord. Before there was the choosing of sides; now there is only one side—God's side. Before there was a sensitive ethnic or racial issue (the kind where no one wins); now there is no issue, and as a result, everyone wins! The Holy Spirit, the executive agent of God, assigned to man to help him triumphantly cope with whatever he encounters, has moved in on the scene.

Likewise the Spirit also helpeth our infirmities: for we know not what we should pray for as we ought: but the Spirit itself maketh intercession for us with groanings which cannot be uttered. And he that searcheth the hearts knoweth what is the mind of the Spirit, because he maketh intercession for the saints according to the will of God. And we know that all things work together for good to them that love God, to them who are the called according to his purpose (Romans 8:26-28).

Undecided in Purpose

On a piece of paper write six terms, three on each side. On the left side write "Super Ego." Underneath it write "Ego." On the third line write "Id." Across from "Super Ego" on the right side write "I ought." Across from "Ego" write "I will." And across from the word "Id" write the words "I want." This is sometimes the psychological explanation for most of the decisions we make. The term *ego* is the ancient Greek word for the capital letter *I*, which we use in the English language. And the term *id* is the Freudian equivalent of what some theologians call the "sin principle."

From the list we see the possibility of a vast difference between what "I want" and what "I ought." Once we understand the process, every time we want something we automatically ask ourselves, "Should I want this particular thing? Is it good for me, or is it bad for me?" Any questionable value judgments are often a warfare between our wants and our oughts. That's where the will comes in. Man's volition takes over, and the decision is made. It is no longer a question of I want or I ought but is now an affirmation "I will!"

The Holy Spirit harmonizes our total being and brings it together under divine control. Of course, when we approach God about our desires, this is perfectly normal. But when we pray about them, we will not have faith enough to receive them unless our desire agrees with God's desire as seen in His Holy Word.

During a conference of the National Association of Evangelicals (NAE) in Orlando, Florida, I served as music director. In the meeting I taught the audience a chorus from John 15:7, "If ye abide in me, and my words abide in you, ye shall ask what ye will, and it shall be done. It shall be done unto you." It's a beautiful Scripture chorus and

71

became one of the favorites of the conference. God used it to minister to that great body of believers gathered from around the world. It indeed illustrates the uniting, harmonizing, orchestrating, symphonizing power of prayer in the life of the body of Christ. John 15:7 is a veritable exegesis of the one mind, one accord and one place mentioned so forcefully in Acts 1:14 and 2:1.

Prayer could be called a big melting pot. When the pot heats up, it will burn out envy, strife, discord, jealousy, malice, hatred, variance and all impurities. Prayer will melt in or make prominent love, joy, peace, long-suffering, gentleness, meekness, faithfulness, goodness and self-control (Galatians 5:19-23). The works of the flesh are forces which totally disorient and confuse the human family. The fruit of the Spirit, however, will unveil the most beautiful portrait of Jesus Christ ever seen by the eyes of man.

Divided in Purpose

In Judges 7 the story of Gideon's army is told in eloquent terms. It is a striking example of how a few who are united are mightier than multitudes who are divided. God's enemies, the Midianites, were described and compared in numbers to grasshoppers and sand of the sea (v. 12). Such a vast army and even the number of camels they possessed seemed impossible to estimate. Judges 8:10 seems to indicate an army of 135,000 Midianites.

Gideon, however, started out with only 32,000 men who had gathered at his call. God told Gideon that this was "too many" and to let those who were "fearful and afraid" leave. Twenty-two thousand went home, leaving only 10,000 to encounter the enemy. God said to Gideon again, "The people are yet too many; bring them down unto the water, and I will try them for thee there" (Judges 7:4). God's test was to set aside every man who at the brook took the water in his hand and lapped it like a dog. Those who bowed down to the water, not looking up so as to watch for the enemy, were sent home. Some 9,700 went home and only 300 remained to fight the enemy.

The 300, less than 1 percent of the original number, were more than enough to defeat God's enemies and win an overwhelming victory for the Lord God of Israel. From the story you will note the 300 were meticulously selected, well disciplined, thoroughly committed and highly organized. The contrast between a united few and a confused horde is pointed out in the final tally of casualties. Not one of the 300 was lost, but 120,000 of the enemy were casualties unto themselves. How clear the Scriptures affirm that with God nothing shall be impossible (Matthew 17:20; Mark 9:23). According to God's mathematics, "And ye shall chase your enemies, and they shall fall before you by the sword. And five of you shall chase an hundred, and an hundred of you shall put ten thousand to flight: and your enemies shall fall before you by the sword" (Leviticus 26:7, 8). In all circumstances it pays to be united. God works in mysterious ways His wonders to perform. When God is working, nothing can hinder. No internal or external forces can defeat us when we are united by God.

Prayer Unites Us in Spirit

God wants us to be together in heart, in soul, in mind and in spirit.

God Deserves a United Church

A united church sings together, prays together, worships together and witnesses together.

And when the day of Pentecost was fully come, they were all with one accord in one place. And suddenly

*there came a sound from heaven as of a rushing mighty
wind, and it filled all the house where they were sitting.
And there appeared unto them cloven tongues like as of
fire, and it sat upon each of them. And they were all
filled with the Holy Ghost, and began to speak with
other tongues, as the Spirit gave them utterance* (Acts
2:1-4).

Unquestionable results accompany united prayer, praise
and adoration. A united church is an interceding church,
a joyful church and a Spirit-filled church. Those who
attend and participate in such a church often remark: "I've
never felt so much love! Everyone really cares and is
concerned for one another."

United Prayer Always Brings Results
The outpouring of the Holy Spirit in Acts 2 is a direct
result of Christ's prayer for unity and sanctification in
John 17. A close look at this marvelous and miraculous
prayer will reveal the immediacy and intensity of our
Lord.

*These words spake Jesus, and lifted up his eyes to heaven,
and said, Father, the hour is come; glorify thy Son, that
thy Son also may glorify thee: As thou hast given him
power over all flesh, that he should give eternal life to as
many as thou hast given him. And this is life eternal,
that they might know thee the only true God, and Jesus
Christ, whom thou hast sent. I have glorified thee on the
earth: I have finished the work which thou gavest me to
do. And now, O Father, glorify thou me with thine own
self with the glory which I had with thee before the world
was. I have manifested thy name unto the men which
thou gavest me out of the world: thine they were, and
thou gavest them me; and they have kept thy word. Now
they have known that all things whatsoever thou hast*

given me are of thee. For I have given unto them the words which thou gavest me; and they have received them, and have known surely that I came out from thee, and they have believed that thou didst send me. I pray for them: I pray not for the world, but for them which thou hast given me; for they are thine. And all mine are thine, and thine are mine; and I am glorified in them. And now I am no more in the world, but these are in the world, and I come to thee. Holy Father, keep through thine own name those whom thou hast given me, that they may be one, as we are. While I was with them in the world, I kept them in thy name: those that thou gavest me I have kept, and none of them is lost, but the son of perdition; that the scripture might be fulfilled. And now come I to thee; and these things I speak in the world, that they might have my joy fulfilled in themselves. I have given them thy word; and the world hath hated them, because they are not of the world, even as I am not of the world. I pray not that thou shouldest take them out of the world, but that thou shouldest keep them from the evil. They are not of the world, even as I am not of the world. Sanctify them through thy truth: thy word is truth. As thou hast sent me into the world, even so have I also sent them into the world. And for their sakes I sanctify myself, that they also might be sanctified through the truth. Neither pray I for these alone, but for them also which shall believe on me through their word; That they all may be one; as thou, Father, art in me, and I in thee, that they also may be one in us: that the world may believe that thou hast sent me. And the glory which thou gavest me I have given them; that they may be one, even as we are one: I in them, and thou in me, that they may be made perfect in one; and that the world may know that thou hast sent me, and hast loved them, as thou hast loved me. Father, I will that they also, whom thou hast given me, be with me where I am; that they may behold my glory, which thou hast given me: for thou lovedst me before the foundation of the world. O righteous Father, the world hath not known thee: but I have known thee, and these have known that thou hast sent me. And I have declared unto them thy name, and will declare it: that the love wherewith thou hast loved me may be in them, and I in them.

"I will send him [Holy Spirit] unto you" (John 16:7). The value of united consistent prayers must not be underestimated. Such prayers always bring results.

Prayer Unites Us in Jesus Christ

"For ye are all the children of God by faith in Christ Jesus. For as many of you as have been baptized into Christ have put on Christ. There is neither Jew nor Greek, there is neither bond nor free, there is neither male nor female: for ye are all one in Christ Jesus. And if ye be Christ's, then are ye Abraham's seed, and heirs according to the promise" (Galatians 3:26-29). To put on Christ means to be clothed with Him, to assume His person and character, and to fulfill the attributes of Christlikeness in daily life by following in His footsteps and doing His works. All races, classes and sexes are one in Christ and equal in rights and privileges in the gospel. They are all one Body with Jesus Christ as the head of the Body. The gulf between Jews and Gentiles, masters and slaves, and male and female has been bridged. The chasm has been spanned and the continents brought together by Christ and the gospel. All Christians are one in unity, in rights, in privileges and benefits, just as the Father, the Son and the Holy Ghost are one in unity.

"For where two or three are gathered together in my name, there am I in the midst of them" (Matthew 18:20).

The power of united prayer is the prayer of the person who is united with Jesus Christ. Jesus said, "If ye abide in me, and my words abide in you, ye shall ask what ye will, and it shall be done unto you" (John 15:7). "Whatsoever ye shall ask of the Father in my name, he may give it you" (v. 16). "Whatsoever ye shall ask the Father in my name, he will give it you" (John 16:23).

Prayer is the uniting force of the universe. It has brought heaven and earth together before and most assuredly is doing so again and again. And one day soon, it will be for all time. *Lord, teach us to pray unitedly.*

Back on the farm at the orphanage, Superintendent C. J. Eller called a group of us boys together and said, "Fellows, this is our *new* John Deere tractor." Wow! Some of us had never seen a tractor before. We had two teams of mules— Pet and Lou, a large team of horse mules, and Sam and Mike, a team of young gray mules. It took us a long time to break the young team. Then again, 120 boys can break most anything. Would you believe that on the first trip into one of our main fields the *new* John Deere tractor got stuck? That's right! Stuck—axle deep in the mud. The two back wheels were taller than I was. At that time I was probably 10 or 11 years old.

Brother Eller said to one of the boys, "Go get Pet and Lou." With a log chain tied to the front axle, Pet and Lou began to pull from a large doubletree harness. Back and forth they jigsawed, Pet pulling on the left and then Lou pulling on the right. Nothing was happening and "John Deere" refused to budge. Brother Eller asked, "Where's Tommy Pitman?" Someone replied, "He's over at the barn." Brother Eller said, "Go get Tommy." Tommy Pitman was one of the older boys who was in charge of the mules. He fed them; he groomed them; he took care of their harness, plowed them in the field and let them out to romp in the big pasture. They knew his voice and his touch.

When Tommy arrived, he analyzed the situation, checked the harness, gave Pet and Lou a couple of strokes, and took the leather plow lines in his hands. After aligning the team and tightening the trace chains, I heard his confident command given simultaneously with the snap of the plow lines. Pet and Lou hit the traces, the doubletree buckled, "John Deere" and the mud gave forth a moan, and that *new* tractor popped up out of the muck and mire like a plastic toy. Every time I review that scene, my mind goes immediately to my first Sunday school class where we used to sing:

If we all pull together, together, together,
If we all pull together, how happy we'll be.
For your work is my work and our work is God's work.
If we all pull together, how happy we'll be.

Prayer
Our Father and our God, how we thank Thee for the lessons You teach us every day. Help us to listen, to learn and to obey. May we never allow ourselves to be divided. May we always stay united. Keep us together in You, in Your love, in Your will and in Your work. This we pray in Jesus' name. Amen.

CHAPTER

—— 6 ——

PRAYING
UNCEASINGLY

Someone has remarked, "A sermon may be eternal without being everlasting." The Christian's correct attitude toward prayer is one of consistent necessity. Dwight D. Eisenhower once said, "Prayer is simply a necessity." By prayer, I mean an effort to get in touch with the infinite. While our supplications are often imperfect, they do bring the finite and the infinite together. This togetherness fosters the necessity of unceasing communication with Divinity. How we need to make time for seeking the mind and heart of God in all matters of life.

For a scriptural foundation, let us underscore the following passages: "Peter therefore was kept in prison: but *prayer* was made without ceasing of the church unto God for him" (Acts 12:5). There are other companion verses. "Without ceasing I make mention of you always in my prayers" (Romans 1:9). "Without ceasing I have remembrance of thee in my prayers night and day" (2 Timothy 1:3) One of the shortest and strongest exhortations is the apostle's emphatic imperative in 1 Thessalonians 5:17, "Pray without ceasing!" In other words, pray always about all things.

The concept of an unceasing tenacity encompasses other

areas of Christian service. First of all, it is found in preaching and teaching. "And *daily* in the temple, and in every house, they ceased not to *teach* and *preach* Jesus Christ" (Acts 5:42).

Second, it is found in the Lord's Prayer, where Jesus taught them to pray, "Give us this day our *daily* bread" (Matthew 6:11).

Third, it is seen in discipleship. Jesus said, "If any man will come after me, let him deny himself, and take up his cross *daily*, and follow me" (Luke 9:23).

Fourth, they gave themselves to the Word of God. "These were more noble than those . . . in that they received the *word* with all readiness of mind, and searched the scriptures *daily*, whether those things were so" (Acts 17:11).

Fifth, they were caught up in the fellowship of the saints and in the winning of souls. "And they, continuing daily with one accord in the temple, and breaking bread from house to house, did eat their meat with gladness and singleness of heart, praising God, and having favor with all the people. And the Lord added to the church daily such as should be saved" (Acts 2:46, 47).

Sixth, it is seen in the shouldering of responsibility. "Beside those things that are without, that which cometh upon me *daily*, the care of all the churches" (2 Corinthians 11:28).

Finally, it is illustrated in the building and encouragement of the body of Christ. "Exhort one another *daily*, while it is called To day; lest any of you be hardened through the deceitfulness of sin" (Hebrews 3:13).

Here is a fourfold formula on how to pray unceasingly: (1) in definition, (2) in the Scriptures, (3) avoiding mockery and derision, (4) in reality.

How to Pray Unceasingly in Definition

The first part of the fourfold formula has to do with defining the terms. What do we mean by praying unceasingly? Most people's first reaction will be, "Why, such an idea is absolutely impossible." And they are probably right if the idea is taken at face value rather than considering the original context and the true meaning of the term which is used.

In the Old Testament, there are basically two words used to clarify the meaning of praying unceasingly. The first is the word *ectenos,* which is a compound word with a prepositional prefix *ec,* meaning "out," and the verb *teno,* which means "to stretch." From these two root words comes the idea of being stretched out. A good illustration to dramatize this point is the pulling of taffy candy. In Gatlinburg, Tennessee, in the heart of the Smoky Mountains, there is a candy factory whose taffy pulling equipment sits in the front window on Main Street. A crowd is generally gathered around, including Mom and Dad and all the kids. It's the greatest advertisement for the mouth watering taffy.

I have often used the pulling of taffy to illustrate the syncopated rhythm of certain styles of gospel music. The first time you pull the candy, it will only stretch so far. The next time, it will probably jump all the way out of gear. It is amazing just how far it will stretch. The longer you pull, the more it will stretch. So keep in mind that one of the New Testament meanings of the word *unceasingly* is "in stretched out fashion."

A companion word to *teno* is the word *teino,* which also means "to stretch," but carries with it the idea of "tension," which is the English derivative. Like a rubber band, the more you pull, the more it stretches and the more tension it acquires. The concept of *intensity* can also be applied to this ongoing and continuous dynamic. "See that ye love one another with a pure heart fervently" (1 Peter 1:22). It means "refusing to let up." Don't relax your effort. Keep doing that which you are doing earnestly, heartily, intensely and consistently with all your strength.

A second New Testament word also has to do with praying unceasingly. It is the word *adialeiptos*. It is used to describe an "incessant heart pain," a gnawing burden, something that is constantly and persistently there. It refuses to let up or give up. Paul says, "I have great heaviness and *continual* sorrow in my heart" (Romans 9:2). Listen to the context from the *Living Bible*.

> *Oh, Israel, my people! Oh, my Jewish brothers! How I long for you to come to Christ. My heart is heavy within me and I grieve bitterly day and night because of you. Christ knows and the Holy Spirit knows that it is no mere pretense when I say that I would be willing to be forever damned if that would save you. God has given you so much, but still you will not listen to him. He took you as his own special, chosen people and led you along with a bright cloud of glory and told you how very much he wanted to bless you. He gave you his rules for daily life so you would know what he wanted you to do. He let you worship him, and gave you mighty promises. Great men of God were your fathers, and Christ himself was one of you, a Jew so far as his human nature is concerned, he who now rules over all things. Praise God forever!* (Romans 9:1-5).

What a powerful scriptural dramatization of the meaning of prayer without ceasing. It is more than a mere unbroken continuity; it *is* being sure prayer is not omitted on any occasion. The burden is incessant, constant and persistent. It is ongoing, ever present, always there. Willie Nelson is not, therefore, the first person to say, "You are always on my mind." In reality, the apostle Paul exclaimed to those whom he loved in the gospel, "You are always in my memory, on my heart, and in my prayers" (see Philippians 1:3, 4). This is more than that which is not interrupted but rather that which is constantly recurring, over and over again. "Remembering without ceasing your work of faith, and labour of love, and patience of hope in our Lord Jesus Christ, in the sight of God and our Father" (1 Thessalonians 1:3). There is a definite wholeness to godly gratitude which recognizes and commends faithful work, loving labor and hopeful patience.

How to Pray Unceasingly in the Scriptures

Having discovered a clearer understanding of the term *without ceasing*, we are now ready to review some actual historical scriptural examples. Few New Testament stories contain greater anticipation and excitement than the one highlighted in our text of Acts 12:5. Simon Peter, one of the great leaders of the early church, was placed in prison. The church had undergone severe persecution, even the slaying of James, the brother of John and the first apostle to be martyred.

Even though it was the time of the religious festival called the Passover, Peter was seized by Herod Agrippa, taken to a maximum security prison and placed under the charge of 16 soldiers—four detachments with four crack guards in each squad who relieved each other four times a day. One commentary said he was chained to two of the soldiers and guarded by two others. It was obvious that Herod intended for Simon Peter to be his prisoner. He was not taking any chance.

"But *prayer* was made *without ceasing* of the church unto God for him" (Acts 12:5). In other words, there was a continual stream of prayer going up to God from the church on his behalf. Clarence Jordan said, "All the while the Rock was being kept in the clink, the fellowship was praying agonizingly for him." On the very night before the day Herod had intended to deliver him up to a kangaroo court, a mock trial and execution, God dispatched a divine delivery diplomat from another world who came down to earth, entered the maximum security prison of Herod Agrippa, walked through gates, guards, walls and all to where the apostle, chained to the guards, was sleeping. The Bible says the angel nudged Peter saying, "Quick! Get up!" While he was doing so, the chains fell off his wrists. "Get dressed and put on your sandals." As he finished, the angel ordered, "Grab your coat and follow me!"

Leaving his cell, Peter looked back on stunned guards and prisoners. *Surely this is a dream*, he thought as he passed the first and second cell block and approached the great iron gate of the prison entrance which opened automatically. Peter, safe and sound on the outside, was led by the angel for about a block down the cobblestone street toward the house where the prayer meeting was being held. When the angel disappeared, Peter said, "It's true! It's really true! The Lord sent His angel and delivered me from Herod and the Jews who wanted to destroy me."

Finding himself at the gate to the house of Mary, the mother of John Mark, Peter rattled the gate, and a damsel named Rhoda came out and immediately ran back inside thinking she had seen a ghost. The praying group couldn't believe her report. Peter, meanwhile, continued knocking. When they finally let him in, their excitement was almost out of control. Finally his presence and gentleness calmed their emotion as he explained in detail his miraculous deliverance from prison in answer to their unceasing prayers. Then he concluded by instructing them to pass the word along to the others also.

It was in the Upper Room that the 120 were praising and

blessing God in one mind, in one place and in one accord. "And when the day of Pentecost was *fully* come . . ." (Acts 2:1). What happened? A spiritual cyclone hit the place, and the marvelous, miraculous initial outpouring of the Holy Spirit was experienced. Jesus had told them in Luke 24:49 to go, wait, tarry, *until*. . . . They obeyed! They did exactly as He commanded. They waited for the promise of the Father. They tarried *until*. They continued in one accord, praising and glorifying God unceasingly. The Bible says, "And *suddenly* there came a sound from heaven as of a rushing mighty wind, and it filled all the house where they were sitting . . . and they were *all* filled with the Holy Ghost" (Acts 2:2, 4). They were determined. The promise was theirs. They would *not* be denied. Each one received a personal Pentecost.

In two parables in the Gospel of Luke, Jesus teaches with great emphasis the lesson that men ought always to pray and not to faint.

> *And he said unto them, Which of you shall have a friend, and shall go unto him at midnight, and say unto him, Friend, lend me three loaves; for a friend of mine in his journey is come to me, and I have nothing to set before him? And he from within shall answer and say, Trouble me not: the door is now shut, and my children are with me in bed; I cannot rise and give thee. I say unto you, Though he will not rise and give him, because he is his friend, yet because of his importunity he will rise and give him as many as he needeth* (Luke 11:5-8).

> *And he spake a parable unto them to this end, that men ought* always *to pray, and not to faint; saying, There was in a city a judge, which feared not God, neither regarded man: and there was a widow in that city; and she came unto him, saying, Avenge me of mine adversary.*

And he would not for a while: but afterward he said within himself, Though I fear not God, nor regard man; yet because this widow troubleth me, I will avenge her, lest by her continual coming she weary me. And the Lord said, Hear what the unjust judge saith. And shall not God avenge his own elect, which cry day and night unto him, though he bear long with them? I tell you that he will avenge them speedily. Nevertheless when the Son of man cometh, shall he find faith on the earth? (Luke 18:1-8).

Prayer without ceasing slowly comes to mean more than quantity and longevity. It now has to do also with quality, intensity and integrity. In Christ's parables we see not only startling opportunity but holy boldness and shamelessness. God desires that we draw nigh unto Him (James 4:8). Not with timidity but with determined self-confidence, knowing *who* we are, *why* we are there and *what* we have come to receive. God delights in an expectant persistence that will not take no for an answer. It is an expression of great faith, and nothing pleases God more than faith. Sometimes God's seeming reticence and hesitance is not that at all but rather His wise fatherly training—teaching us lessons we could not learn otherwise. What astute parent gives to his child at every first asking and showers him with everything he desires? Could it be that God is often trying, testing, weighing or proving in order to temper the true strength of the metal and timber in one's character? Do we mean business with God? Are we only on an experimental excursion into the fantasy land of religious glamour? God has His own ways of whisking away the chafe in order to salvage the pure grain of the wheat.

Could it be that God enjoys the tenacity of importunity? That continual knocking until the hesitant neighbor gets up, lights a candle and gives his suppliant not one piece of bread but every loaf in the house in order to get him out of there so he can go back to sleep? The point is well-documented in sacred Scripture. Over and over we see unceasing supplication, continuous knocking, habitual seeking and spontaneous asking. "Ye have not because ye ask not" (James 4:2). "Ask, and it shall be given you; seek, and ye shall find; knock, and it shall be opened unto you: for every one that asketh receiveth; and he that seeketh findeth; and to him that knocketh it shall be opened" (Matthew 7:7, 8).

Even in the Old Testament there are numerous occasions of similar action. Genesis 18:23-32 records the account of Abraham's encounter with God concerning the ultimate destruction of Sodom and Gomorrah. Abraham had a point, and he moved the heart of God. In Genesis 32:24-29 Jacob wrestled with an angel until the early morning hours saying, "I will *not* let go, *until* you bless me." In Exodus 32:10 God told Moses, "I'm going to destroy Israel." Moses, responding as their spiritual leader and pastor, said, "If so, then blot my name out of your book" (see Exodus 32:32). Start with me, strike through my name first. Put me at the head of the line and destroy me first! It reminded me of John Knox who prayed, "Lord give me Scotland or I die." Some Christians have even prayed, "Lord, save my companion, children, and loved ones, even if it means the taking of my own life." The scriptural admonition to pray without ceasing includes not only continuity but intensity and integrity.

How to Pray Unceasingly and Avoid Mockery

Why is it that some never have a prayer until they first have a care? Is it possible that most use prayer as a spare tire, only in case of emergencies. With the new modern puncture-proof, mileage-guaranteed radial tires, we rarely ever realize the presence of a spare tire in the trunk of our vehicle unless we hear a strange noise and the car starts swaying out of control. So many have only "spare-tire" religion and know very little about true salvation. To use prayer only in cases of emergency is a mockery of God.

The playing of religion and making sport of eternal principles is blasphemy. Proverbs 1:22-32 describes the feeling of God toward such impropriety. In the New Testament mockery is directed toward Christ by the Pharisees in Luke 16:14 and by the rulers at the Crucifixion in Luke 23:35. Galatians 6:7 sums it up, "Be not deceived; God is not mocked: for whatsoever a man soweth, that shall he also reap." Make no mistake about it, you cannot cheat on God. God will not be intimidated. Proverbs intimates, "If you mock me, I will mock you. Ignore me and I will ignore you. If you play games with me, I will have no alternative but to play the same game with you. Don't be under any illusion. You can't make a fool of God! Your mockery is not of God—He cannot be mocked. Your mockery is of yourself and your posterity." A man's harvest in life will depend entirely on what he sows.

Sometime ago I read of a certain individual who kept a plaque of the Lord's Prayer hanging on the wall at his bedside. Every night when he retired they said he would point with his finger toward the plaque and say, "Those are my sentiments, Lord, exactly." And into bed he would go. What a time to evaluate our prayer life—especially in light of the exhortation "to *pray* without ceasing." If man's physical diet were rationed in proportion to his spiritual serving, the whole Christian world would seem like Biafra and Ethiopia. Far too many have forgotten Christ's example "Give us *this day* our *daily* bread." *Lord, teach us to pray unceasingly!*

How to Pray Unceasingly in Reality

Have you ever awakened in the wee hours of the morning praying, worshiping, praising, rejoicing and calling upon God? I've tried to figure it out by analyzing what has happened. I didn't plan it that way. It just happened. Many of us often pray ourselves to sleep, so it's no wonder we wake ourselves up praying also. There are times, however, when our subconscious minds seem to take over, and unctionized by the Holy Spirit, the inner self—real you—does things that we are not consciously aware of. Suddenly it becomes so powerful and real we cannot help being aware of the presence and essence of communion with Divinity.

Oh, how we need to maintain an open line of communication and constant contact with God. Don't ever sever that blessed relationship. Don't ever allow the connection to become broken or disallowed. My son belongs to the Volunteer Firemen in his community. In order to stay in touch and be ready for a call to action, he wears a beeper. It is amazing how much and how many are saved from fires because the lines of communications are always open. In a definite sense, this world is on fire, and we are God's volunteer firemen. Let's keep the lines of communications *open. Lord, teach us to pray unceasingly!*

Prayer

We thank Thee, our heavenly Father, that You are a very present help in the time of need. We are grateful that You can be touched with the feeling of our infirmities. Such eternal vigilance and unhindered accessibility compounds our sense of Your omnipresence. May we take full advantage of such a privilege by praying, believing and receiving from You, in Jesus' name. Amen.

CHAPTER

7

PRAYING
EFFECTIVELY

The dictionary gives an example of the word *effectual*: "Quinine is an effectual preventative of malaria." Effectual means to be valid or to be effective. To be effectual means to produce the desired effect. So you might say that an effectual prayer is effective. "The effectual fervent prayer of a righteous man availeth much" (James 5:16).

Consider five positive results of a successful prayer life: (1) A biblical prayer life will affect the heart of God. (2) It will call in all the resources of heaven. (3) It will affect the person for whom you are praying. (4) It will affect the problem about which you are praying. (5) It will affect the person doing the praying.

Prayer Will Affect the Heart of God

God said to Moses, "Let me alone, that I may destroy them, and blot out their name from under heaven: and I will make of thee a nation mightier and greater than they" (Deuteronomy 9:14).

Then Moses gives this account: "As at the first, forty days and forty nights: I did neither eat bread, nor drink water, because of all your sins. . . . For I was afraid of the anger and hot displeasure, wherewith the Lord was wroth against you to destroy you. But the Lord hearkened unto me at that time also. And the Lord was very angry with Aaron to have destroyed him: and I prayed for Aaron also the same time."

The prayer which Moses prayed is found in Exodus 32:32: "Yet now, if thou wilt forgive their sin—; and if not, blot me, I pray thee, out of thy book which thou has written."

There were several previous incidents that necessitated this prayer. After leading the children of Israel out of Egypt, Moses had turned the congregation over to Aaron, his brother, and said to him, "Aaron, the people must have a leader. You take charge of things while I go to the mountain in order to be with God and to beseech Him on behalf of this nation."

So Moses went to the mountain to receive the message God had for the people. During this special time a number of things happened. God came down and wrote His Law in 10 particular writings on tablets. The Scripture says the finger of God came down and wrote the Law of God on tablets hewed out of the side of the mountain and God gave them to Moses. Moses said to God, "I want to see You!" But God said, "You can't see Me. However, if you'll cover yourself in the cleft of the rock, I'll put My hand over the place where you're hiding, and when I pass by you'll not be able to look on My face, but you will be able to see My hinder parts."

As God passed by, Moses was in His presence. When he came down from the mountain, he had so much of the glory of God upon his countenance that the people couldn't look directly at him and begged him to cover his face. As James L. Slay puts it, "The glory of God was oozing out of the pores of his skin."

God said to Moses, "Get back down to your people quickly for they have defiled themselves." With the tablets in his hand, Moses came down off the mountain. When he came within view of the people and saw how they had corrupted themselves, he became very angry and flung the tablets to the ground, breaking them into pieces just as the laws of God had been shattered by the flagrant sin and overt transgression of the people.

The tablets were no more broken than was the heart of God and the heart of their spiritual leader. When Moses saw what had happened, his grief was compounded because his own brother, Aaron, had been corrupted also. Moses, however, maintained his equilibrium by the means of consistent prayer. He said to God, "If you won't forgive them or spare them, then start with me, take my name out first, blot my name also out of your book."

Was that an effective prayer? Indeed it was, for it touched the heart of God at an unusual time. It is a dramatic illustration of how the heart of God can be touched and how the mind of God can be changed. Even though a Sovereign God was justified in desiring to do what He wanted to do, yet the prayer of a man touched the heart of God and a nation was saved from destruction. There is no better way to come nearer to the heart of God than by the means of prayer.

> There is a place of quiet rest,
> Near to the heart of God,
> A place where sin cannot molest,
> Near to the heart of God.
> Oh, Jesus, blest redeemer,
> Sent from the heart of God,
> Hold us who wait before Thee
> Near to the heart of God.
> —Cleland B. McAfee

Prayer Will Call in All the Resources of Heaven
Prayer will affect the heart of God and call in all the

resources of heaven. Ours is a computerized age. If we have access to a computer and have a problem that needs to be solved, we feed that problem into the computer. The computer then goes to work using all its resources, bringing together all of its data to resolve the particular problem. It gives us not only our answer but options and alternatives related to that problem.

Through the miracle of prayer, we have access to a "divine computer." We can bring our needs and our problems to the Lord. Once they are fed into the heart and mind of God, all the resources of heaven and the universe for time and eternity are at His disposal.

"What things soever ye desire, when ye pray, believe that ye receive them, and ye shall have them" (Mark 11:24).

"Prove me now herewith, saith the Lord of hosts, if I will not open you the windows of heaven, and pour you out a blessing, that there shall not be room enough to receive it" (Malachi 3:10).

Through prayer, finite men and women have all the resources of an infinite God. Is it any wonder He works in mysterious ways His wonders to perform? Is it any wonder He turns stumbling blocks into stepping-stones, defeat into triumph and impossibilities into possibilities? When God is at work, no man can hinder. God is made accessible to us through the power of prayer. Jesus said, "With men this is impossible; but with God all things are possible" (Matthew 19:26). "Jesus said unto him, If thou canst believe, all things are possible to him that believeth" (Mark 9:23).

Moses and Israel had a range of mountains to the north and a range of mountains to the south. The Red Sea was before them and an army of Egyptians was hot on their heels, led by a mad Pharaoh in wild pursuit and wanting to bury them in the sea or take them back to the brickyards of Goshen. What normal person could possibly find a solution to such an impossible situation? Moses, knowing God would intervene, exclaimed, "Stand still, and see the salvation of the Lord!" Extending the rod that God had taught him to use in the desert, Moses watched as the sea parted and God's people marched through the Red Sea all the way to the other side on dry ground.

Pharaoh's army came along and decided they, too, would go through on dry ground. But God had something else in mind. Pharaoh and his hoards ran out of dry ground. Moses called on the resources of heaven, and it was more than enough for the task. Is it any wonder Miriam grabbed her tambourine and started singing, shouting and praising Jehovah God?

"Eye hath not seen, nor ear heard, neither have entered into the heart of man, the things which God hath prepared for them that love him" (1 Corinthians 2:9).

What resources were available to Joshua as he started out in a battle and wondered, "How in the world are we going to win? The enemy has more ammunition, more equipment and more soldiers." Suddenly the clouds in the sky changed colors, and it began to rain. The rain became hail—so large it killed people. When the battle was over and they counted the casualties, more men had died from the hail from heaven than from the swords of the trained soldiers.

What resources are available to the child of God through prayer! Joshua could tell us about another similar occasion when he needed more time to finish the battle. He was winning the battle but running out of daylight. If only he had a few more hours of fighting time—if only he could turn back the clock! How on earth could it be possible? He couldn't turn on the floodlights like we do in the stadiums and arenas today. What he did is found in Joshua 10:12-14: "Sun, stand thou still upon Gibeon; and thou, Moon, in the valley of Ajalon. And the sun stood still, and the moon stayed, until the people had avenged themselves upon their enemies. Is not this written in the book of Jasher? So the sun stood still in the midst of heaven, and hasted not to go down about a whole day. And there was no day like that before it or after it, that *the Lord hearkened unto the voice of a man: for the Lord fought for Israel.*"

Prayer—effectual prayer—makes available the resources of heaven. What resources? Amazing and unthought-of resources are accessible to God's people through the power of prayer.

"Is anything too hard for the Lord" (Genesis 18:14). This question is appropriately answered by Vep Ellis in the words of his song: "My God can do anything. Anything? Anything!" I wondered why there were so many *anythings*. The first one is a statement. The second one is a question. And the third one is an answer.

> My God can do anything.
> He made the earth with all its fullness,
> And all that time shall bring.
> My God can do anything.
> —Vep Ellis

Prayer Will Affect the People for Whom We Are Praying

Prayer will not only touch the heart of God and call in the resources of heaven, it will also impact the individual for whom you are praying. In Genesis 20:17, Abraham prayed for Abimelech and he, his wife, and his household were healed. Moses prayed for his brother, Aaron, and he was spared (Deuteronomy 9:20). Hannah prayed for a son and received a son (1 Samuel 1:10, 27). Job prayed for his friends and both he and his friends were restored (Job 42:7, 8, 10). Jesus prayed for Simon Peter that his faith would not fail and that Satan would not be able to sift him as wheat (Luke 22:31, 32). The disciples prayed before choosing a successor for Judas Iscariot and Mathias was chosen (Acts

1:24). Peter prayed for Tabitha and she was raised from the dead (Acts 9:40). Throughout the Scriptures the needs of countless people were supplied through the power of prayer. God is in the people business—all people. He is "no respecter of persons" (Acts 10:34).

In Lawrenceville, Georgia, I pastored a wonderful congregation for four exciting years. During the first year the Men's Prayer Fellowship met at the church early every Saturday morning and made a list of requests in a little pocket spiral notebook. The list was ongoing from Saturday to Saturday. As God answered, we would mark the request off; otherwise, we continued to pray. One name I remember writing down—a husband, a father, a son, a brother, a backslider, a former member of the church. His name was one of the first on a four-year list. And during the fourth year of our pastorate, he was gloriously restored to faith in the Lord Jesus Christ. God still answers prayer. He still answers personal prayers, and He still answers prayers prayed for other people.

When Nicky Cruz preached in my pulpit in Nashville, Tennessee, Helen and I knew the validity of his testimony. We were there in New York City with Dave Wilkerson when many of the things happened as recorded in *The Cross and the Switchblade*. We witnessed personally on the streets and in the parks. We prayed long and hard with the young people and with a wonderful staff of dedicated Christians committed to that ministry. God still answers specific personal prayers that change people.

Prayer Will Affect the Problems and Circumstances About Which You Are Wrestling
Elijah prayed that it *not* rain, and the Bible said it did not rain for three and a half years. Again he prayed, and the heavens were opened and the earth brought forth her fruit (James 5:17, 18). Elijah also prayed for fire to fall from

heaven and consume the sacrifice which he had prepared as a challenge to the false prophet, Baal. The Bible says, "Then the *fire* of the Lord fell and consumed the burnt-sacrifice" (1 Kings 18:38), proving beyond a doubt that God will, if necessary, go to great lengths to answer the effectual fervent prayer of a righteous person. Prayer will affect political and theological problems. Prayer can even affect the weather.

> *I love the LORD, because he hath heard my voice and my supplications. Because he hath inclined his ear unto me, therefore will I call upon him as long as I live. The sorrows of death compassed me, and the pains of hell gat hold upon me: I found trouble and sorrow. Then called I upon the name of the LORD; O LORD, I beseech thee, deliver my soul. Gracious is the LORD, and righteous; yea, our God is merciful. The LORD preserveth the simple: I was brought low, and he helped me. Return unto thy rest, O my soul; for the LORD hath dealt bountifully with thee* (Psalm 116:1-7).

> *Unto thee, O LORD, do I lift up my soul. O my God, I trust in thee: let me not be ashamed, let not mine enemies triumph over me. Yea, let none that wait on thee be ashamed: let them be ashamed which transgress without cause. Shew me thy ways, O LORD; teach me thy paths. Lead me in thy truth, and teach me: for thou art the God of my salvation; on thee do I wait all the day* (Psalm 25:1-5).

Prayer is important all day and every day. "Pray for one another, that ye may be healed" (James 5:16). "Pray ye therefore the Lord of the harvest, that he will send forth labourers into his harvest" (Matthew 9:38). "Pray for them which despitefully use you, and persecute you" (Matthew 5:44). Jesus prayed prior to His preaching in the next town (Mark 1:35, 38). In Luke 5:16, He prayed and in verse 17,

"The power of the Lord was present to heal." In the Garden of Gethsemane He prayed, "Remove this cup from me; nevertheless, not my will but thine be done" (Luke 22:42). "And there appeared an angel unto him from heaven, strengthening him" (v. 43). Prayer is the prescription for every problem. Prayer is probably *the* most effective and powerful privilege God has ever granted to us. *Lord, teach us to pray effectively.*

Prayer Affects the Person Doing the Praying

This concept hadn't dawned on me until recently. I knew prayer affected many things, but I never realized how far-reaching its power was. Suddenly it came to me—prayer also affects the one doing the praying. A revised version of this particular passage says, "The supplication of a righteous man availeth much in its working" *(ASV)*, meaning in its "in-working." Such prayer is not only going out and going up, the power of that prayer is also working somewhere else. It is producing an effect inside the praying person, bringing him in line with the will, purpose and plan of Almighty God. "For it is God which worketh in you both to will and to do of his good pleasure" (Philippians 2:13).

Working in you, indeed! God is working in you, on you and through you. A divine operation is going on in the souls of mankind. That's why we need to quit holding back—let go and let God work! As His instruments and His vessels we can be used of God to His honor and His glory. "And there are diversities of operations, but it is the same God which worketh all in all" (1 Corinthians 12:6).

God is working in all directions both to will and to do. This operation reminds me of what medical science calls "microsurgery." They say that with modern-day computerized equipment, they can actually do stitches on something the size of a pinhead. This seems almost unbelievable!

Likewise is the Holy Spirit's operation—intricate, immaculate, minute and miraculous. When we wonder sometimes why this or that doesn't happen, let us keep in mind that God is working according to a plan, blueprint and a scheme He has laid out.

Tennyson wrote, "More things are wrought by prayer than this world dreams of." For years I never had any idea that my prayers would affect me. I knew they certainly seemed to affect everything else. Prayer affects God; it affects the resources of heaven. It affects the person and the problem. And perhaps most importantly of all—it affects you and me every time we pray.

The effectual prayer is an effective prayer. It works! Why not allow the power of prayer to work on you?

Prayer

Father, over and over again Your Word keeps coming, probing, working and doing Your will in our lives. I want to thank You for the hunger You have placed in all of our hearts to know more about You. Thank You for all who love Your Word, receive it, apply it, believe it and act upon it.

Yes, Lord, "we can hear the sound of abundance of rain." We can hear the sound of a going in the mulberry trees. We believe the showers of blessings and torrents of Your grace are on the way.

Thank You also, Father, for the sinner who knows the worth of prayer. Speak to his heart. Speak to the backslider who has grown cold and indifferent. Touch each of us with a hot coal of fire from off the altar of God. Make us new! Bring revival to the hearts of the people. This I pray in Jesus' name, Amen.

CHAPTER

———8———

PRAYING
REVERENTLY

J ust as reverence is a sign of strength, irreverence is a sure indication of weakness. Sometimes we are unconsciously irreverent because of our lack of understanding of reverence. Let us lay a foundation by reviewing a few scriptural passages and considering the possibility of irreverence.

Jesus himself became very upset at the circumstance which He encountered in John 2:13-17:

> *And the Jews' passover was at hand, and Jesus went up to Jerusalem. And found in the temple those that sold oxen and sheep and doves, and the changers of money sitting: And when he had made a scourge of small cords, he drove them all out of the temple, and the sheep, and the oxen; and poured out the changers' money and overthrew the tables; And said unto them that sold doves, Take these things hence; make not my Father's house an house of merchandise. And his disciples remembered that it was written, The zeal of thine house hath eaten me up.*

First of all, the occasion started out to be "the Lord's Passover" (Exodus 12:11, 17; Leviticus 23:5; Numbers 28:16), but now it degenerated to the designation "the Jew's passover" (John 2:13; 6:4; 11:55). What had originally been "the feasts of the Lord" (Leviticus 23:2) had now become the "feast of the Jews" (John 5:1; 6:4; 7:2; 11:56; 19:42). Even the *commandments* of the Lord were nullified and replaced by the *traditions* of men (Matthew 15:1-9, 16:6-12). "It is written, My house shall be called the house of prayer; but ye have made it a den of thieves" (Matthew 21:13). Jesus had a consuming concern that all men respect the things of God.

"The fear of the Lord is the beginning of knowledge: but fools despise wisdom and instruction" (Proverbs 1:7). The *Living Bible* asks the question, "How does a man become wise? The first step is to trust and reverence the Lord! Only fools refuse to be taught."

Three words in this passage cry out for exposition. First of all, the word *fear* means "religious reverence, homage and awe." Second, the word *beginning* refers to the initial principle and *not* the end of knowledge. True wisdom is to justify God even to the condemnation of self. The word *fools* can be explained in three terms: (1) to be evil, lax or exhibiting a careless habit of mind and body; to be perverse, silly and a fool; (2) to be fast, dense or stupid, manifesting foolishness in impiety; (3) to be vulgar, lewd and a lowbred scaly creature. Solomon is here showing the advantage of acting according to the dictates of wisdom and the dangers of acting contrary to them. True reverence is *not* the end but the beginning of knowledge.

"Ye shall keep my sabbaths, and reverence my sanctuary: I am the Lord" (Leviticus 19:30). The Bible has always stood strongly and firmly against Sabbath breaking and the desecration of the Lord's Day. Any violation of God's will and purposes is irreverent. Many are the commands to keep holy unto the Lord: His worship, His day and His place. Why? Because of our tendency to neglect those commands and to break God's sacred laws, because of our temptation to substitute something else in its place and to rationalize our choices as being equally important. The word *worship*, for instance, comes from the root word *worth*. We worship that which has the highest value, essence and meaning in our lives, that which holds first place in our conscious thoughts and even in our waking hours. Obedience and respect for a sovereign God was foremost in Jewish thought and action.

"Now when Mephibosheth, the son of Jonathan, the son of Saul, was come unto David, he fell on his face, and did reverence" (2 Samuel 9:7). Mephibosheth was the crippled son of Jonathan, son of King Saul. David and Jonathan were the best of friends, probably as close, or closer, than brothers. When David became King after Saul, Mephibosheth's grandfather, normally all of the former dynasty's household would have been slain and their possessions destroyed or confiscated as spoils. However, when David became the king, he decreed that Mephibosheth would not only be spared but also become a member of the king's family. When the blessing was pronounced upon the deposed, handicapped prince, he was so overwhelmed by the king's generosity that he fell prostrate in David's presence, doing obeisance by bowing his face to the ground. David immediately set Mephibosheth at ease and welcomed him into his household as a son.

There are four additional passages I want to group together showing those who reverence and those who do not:

"Then Bathsheba bowed with her face to the earth, did reverence to the king, and said, 'Let my lord king David live for ever' " (1 Kings 1:31).

"And all the king's servants, that were in the king's gate, bowed, and reverenced Haman: for the king had so commanded concerning him. But Mordecai bowed not, nor did him reverence" (Esther 3:2).

"God is greatly to be feared in the assembly of the saints, and to be had in reverence of all them that are about him" (Psalm 89:7).

"Serve God acceptably with reverence and godly fear" (Hebrews 12:28).

When King David proclaimed Solomon, his son, as the successor to his throne, Bathsheba, Solomon's mother, responded appropriately. Mordecai, like Daniel, would only bow down in reverence to God, who was the only true God of the ages and of the universe.

One of the strongest and most vivid passages on irreverence is Luke 20:13: "Then said the lord of the vineyard, what shall I do? I will send my beloved son: it may be they will reverence him when they see him." Most of us know the rest of the story. They did *not* reverence his son; they murdered him, even as they crucified God's only begotten Son, Jesus, who became our Savior and our Lord. It is because of the horrendous sin of irreverence and the great importance of reverence that I emphasize it as an important part of prayer. After this strong scriptural introduction, consider the following three points: (1) a reverent approach, (2) a tactful appeal and (3) a grateful acceptance.

A Reverent Approach

Approach God With Reverence

No man will rise high who jeers at sacred things. Reverence is a noble sentiment. It is degrading for the vulgar mind to escape the sense of its own littleness by elevating itself and being antagonistic toward that which is above it. He who has no pleasure in looking up is not fit to look down. Always and in everything let there be reverence. A man who bows down to nothing can never bear the burden of himself. Revere the majesty of God. Fear God, and you have nothing else to fear. The soul of the Christian religion is reverence. Reverence for the things of God must be taught as well as "caught." Reverence controls behavior. Behavior does not control reverence.

Oliver Wendell Holmes once said, "I have in my heart a small, shy plant called reverence. I cultivate it every Sunday morning." We treat God with irreverence when we banish Him from our thoughts and admit Him only into certain areas which we call sacred. He must be Lord of all, or He will not be Lord at all! Shakespeare exclaimed in one of his plays, "Rather let my head stoop to the block than my knees bow to any, save the God of heaven."

Reverence is the very first element of religion. It can only be felt by those who have right views of divine greatness and the right view of their own character in the sight of God. To revere is to love, to respect deeply, to honor greatly, to stand back as in awe. Even the idea of fear as seen in the Old and New Testaments implies deep respect mixed with love, wonder and awe. The root idea is that of falling down in total prostration, moving toward another in humility, realizing that the one toward whom we are moving is superior and above all. *Lord, teach us to pray reverently!*

Approach God With Singing

"Come before his presence with singing" (Psalm 100:2). How I love to open a worship service with music and with singing! Helen and I can walk into a church and hear the people worshiping in singing, and instantly we are in the presence of God.

"And they ministered before the dwelling place of the tabernacle of the congregation with singing" (1 Chronicles 6:32).

"And David and all Israel played before God with all

their might, and with singing, and with harps, and with psalteries, and with timbrels, and with cymbals, and with trumpets" (1 Chronicles 13:8).

Music is a part of nature. Music is a part of life. Music is a part of God. Music is a part of the church. Music will be a part of heaven. Jesus came to set our hearts to singing. He came to tune us up, to bring order out of chaos, harmony out of confusion and music out of discord. "In the midst of the church will I sing praise unto thee" (Hebrews 2:12). "And at midnight Paul and Silas prayed, and sang praises unto God" (Acts 16:25, 26). Not only does singing bring us into His presence, it also brings God into our midst as well.

Approach God With Thanksgiving
"Enter into his gates with thanksgiving, and into his courts with praise: be thankful unto him, and bless his name. For the Lord is good; his mercy is everlasting; and his truth endureth to all generations" (Psalm 100:4, 5).

Thanksgiving means acknowledging and confessing, with gladness, the benefits and mercies which God so bountifully bestows upon us and others. "I exhort therefore, that, first of all, supplications, prayers, intercessions, and giving of thanks, be made for all men; For kings, and for all that are in authority; that we may lead a quiet and peaceable life in all godliness and honesty. For this is good and acceptable in the sight of God our Saviour" (1 Timothy 2:1-3).

"In every thing by prayer and supplication with thanksgiving let your requests be made known unto God" (Philippians 4:6).

Approach God With Praise
"Enter into his courts with . . . praise" (Psalm 100:4). "For great is the Lord and greatly to be praised" (1 Chronicles 16:25). "I will bless the Lord at all times: his

praise shall continually be in my mouth" (Psalm 34:1). "Whoso offereth praise glorifieth me" (Psalm 50:23). "Out of the mouths of babes and sucklings thou hast perfected praise" (Matthew 21:16).

Approach God With Your Need

"Then cometh Jesus from Galilee to Jordan unto John, to be baptized of him. But John forbad him, saying, I have need to be baptized of thee" (Matthew 3:13, 14). Robert Schuller loves to say, "Find a hurt and heal it, find a need and fill it."

When we were out west in the missions states, any help we received came from the tithe of tithes sent to International Headquarters. One day after encountering an urgent need, I wrote a letter of request to the General Overseer, who at that time was Charles W. Conn. The Executive Committee met, considered my request and declined it because of a lack of funds. Their letter read, "We are declining your request. Please do not ask again."

The next week I was scheduled to be in Cleveland for an Evangelism and Home Missions Board meeting. I made an appointment with the general overseer and prepared a second letter of appeal. While sitting facing Dr.Conn, he said to me, "Ben, don't you read your mail, son?" And I said, "Yes sir." He questioned, "Didn't we decline your request and tell you not to submit it to us again?" I replied, "Yes sir, you sure did, Brother Conn. And I read every word of that letter over and over again, but it still hasn't changed the need. The need is still there. We still need someone to help us. And I'm here in person on behalf of that need." My request was granted. There was a need.

Whenever there is a need, I have no timidity or hesitancy in believing that God is going to help us. He didn't say He would supply our wants, but He did say He would "supply all your need according to his riches in glory by Christ Jesus" (Philippians 4:19).

Lord, teach us to pray reverently, to approach you with singing, with praise, with thanksgiving and with genuine need.

A Tactful Appeal

"For we have not an high priest which cannot be touched with the feeling of our infirmities; but was in all points tempted like as we are, yet without sin. Let us therefore come boldly unto the throne of grace, that we may obtain mercy, and find grace to help in time of need" (Hebrews 4:15, 16).

The word *touched* is from the original word *sum-patheo*, where we get the word *sympathize*. How does God feel about us? Matthew 8:17 answers, "Himself took our infirmities, and bare our sicknesses." This word *took* is from the word *lambano*, which means "to take, in order to carry away." The word *bare* means "to lift, with the idea of removal." Then there is the word *nasa*, which means "to bare, or to take the debt of sin and sickness upon oneself and carry it as his own."

"Surely he hath borne our griefs, and carried our sorrows: yet we did esteem him stricken, smitten of God, and afflicted" (Isaiah 53:4). Sympathy means "to suffer with another." Empathy projects one's own consciousness into the consciousness of another. As the Indian man put it, "Walk a mile in my moccasins." Jesus not only stepped into our shoes, He became one of us. Let us therefore come boldly! Since the identification is so complete and so genuine, He does not want us to hold back. The reverent approach and the tactful appeal is one of boldness.

"Let us draw near with a true heart in full assurance of faith" (Hebrews 10:22). "Draw nigh to God, and he will draw nigh to you" (James 4:8).

Dale Carnegie once defined the word *tact* as "being able to gather honey without turning over the hive." If you've ever seen anyone gather honey, you've seen a person with strength, boldness and finesse. They go about their task with confidence and assurance yet with gentleness. There is no panic. Panic turns over the hive. *Lord, teach us a reverent approach and a tactful appeal!*

A Grateful Acceptance

The Lord Giveth and the Lord Taketh Away

"The Lord gave, and the Lord hath taken away; blessed be the name of the Lord" (Job 1:21).

Some years ago I was privileged to work with the Rev. W.C. Byrd, who was then the overseer of Tennessee. I was serving that state as director of youth and Christian education. I learned so much from Brother and Sister Byrd and their family. I often find myself quoting some of his sayings. His philosophy of life was so down-to-earth and so real. He used to say, "If I don't get what I want, I want what I get." This stuck in my mind and I thought, *There's no way to lose with this kind of philosophy—you're always a winner.*

Someone has said God answers prayer in one of three ways. Sometimes He says, "Yes!" Sometimes He says, "No!" And other times He says, "Wait a while." But He always answers one way or the other. "The Lord gave, and the Lord hath taken away; blessed be the name of the Lord" (Job 1:21).

My mother died when she was only 29; at that time I was about 7 or 8 years old. People have often asked me, "Bennie, would you bring your mother back if you could?" And I answer, "No." You see, I know she lived a Christian life and I know about the deprivations she suffered. The autopsy showed that she had multiple surgeries for cancer and numerous other complications. Yes, the lab report said "terminal disease," but my heart and mind always said "malnutrition." My diet was the same as hers with the important exception that she often went without so that we could have something to eat. I would not have made it had I not been placed in the Church of God Home for Children. I would not bring her back because I know my mom is in a much better place and that her suffering is over. *Lord, teach us to pray reverently!*

Teach Us a Grateful Acceptance of Your Word and Your Will in All Things

Like Job, "Though God slay me," or as Charles Conn has put it, "Though God stab me, and I see Him do it, yet will I trust Him!"

Isaiah grew up helping care for the church house. One day while he was in the temple, something happened to him as described in Isaiah 6. God's presence filled the temple, and Isaiah realized it. He responded to it by falling prostrate and crying out, "Woe is me, for I am undone. I am a man of unclean lips" (Isaiah 6:5). An angel took tongs and a hot coal from off the altar of God and touched his lips and proclaimed that Isaiah had been cleansed. Then Isaiah began to hear God talking. Prayer is not only our talking to God but God talking to us.

If we expect God to listen to us, we need to learn to listen to Him. When God and man listen to one another, it is not long until they begin to respond to one another. Isaiah heard God saying, "Whom shall I send and who will go for us?" (v. 8). I don't believe there is any one of us who could experience what Isaiah experienced without responding exactly as he responded, "Here am I, Lord, send me!" He had a reverent approach, a tactful appeal and a grateful acceptance. *Lord, teach us to pray reverently.*

Prayer

Father, we just praise, honor and glorify Your name for the special times when we can sit together around Your table as You break the bread and we receive the nourishment which You have provided. Thank You for the power, strength and ability to resist the evil that comes against us. Thank You for making us able to cope and to be more than conquerors.

We submit ourselves to Your lordship and stand in awe of Your glory, holiness and sovereignty. May Your will be done in our lives. Teach us by Your Word and guide us by Your Holy Spirit, in Jesus' name. Amen.

CHAPTER

9

PRAYING
FERVENTLY

The same text used for the topic "How to Pray Effectively" may also be applied to praying fervently: "Confess your faults one to another, and pray one for another, that ye may be healed. The effectual fervent prayer of a righteous man availeth much" (James 5:16). While studying the intricacies of prayer, I discovered that prayer works not only inwardly and outwardly but upwardly as well. Someone has wisely said, "Prayer works!" Indeed, prayer works, and it ofttimes works when nothing else will.

Since this text extols not only the effectual prayer but also the fervent prayer, and since we are Pentecostal as well as Evangelical, why not inject a little fire and enthusiasm into the ministry of intercession? To be Pentecostal would automatically suggest the flame, fire and fervor which the Holy Spirit brings. As John the Baptist exclaimed in Matthew 3:11, "He [Jesus] shall baptize you with the Holy Ghost, and with fire." "And there appeared unto them cloven tongues like as of fire, and it sat upon each of them. And they were all filled with the Holy Ghost" (Acts 2:3, 4).

Let us examine four aspects of praying fervently: (1) how to pray with a fervent spirit, (2) how to pray with a fervent mind, (3) how to pray with a fervent love and (4) how to pray fervent prayers. We will begin with an introduction of what is meant by the concept of fervency plus a discussion of the natural and spiritual results of fire.

Introduction

Fire can hurt and destroy; it can also warm, sooth and comfort. Fire can energize and inspire, purify and refine, reveal and try.

In the Scriptures fire is seen as an indication of God's presence. "And the angel of the Lord appeared unto him [Moses] in a flame of fire out of the midst of a bush: and he looked, and, behold, the bush burned with fire, and the bush was not consumed" (Exodus 3:2). "And mount Sinai was altogether on a smoke, because the Lord descended upon it in fire: and the smoke thereof ascended as the smoke of a furnace, and the whole mount quaked greatly" (Exodus 19:18). "And the sight of the glory of the Lord was like devouring fire on the top of the mount in the eyes of the children of Israel" (Exodus 24:17). How we need the presence of God in our midst! How we need to understand that praying ground is holy ground! God's presence drives out the darkness and brings in the light. In some cases God may even need to shake us up a bit in order to wake us out of our lethargy and ease in Zion.

Fire also accompanied the offering of sacrifices to God. "It is a burnt offering unto the Lord: it is a sweet savour, an offering made by fire unto the Lord" (Exodus 29:18). It is in prayer that our total being is placed anew and afresh upon the altar of the Lord. Oh, that our praise and adoration might be a sweet smelling savor unto the Lord and our offering always acceptable in His sight! No wonder Paul wrote, "I beseech you therefore, brethren, by the mercies of God, that ye present your bodies a living sacrifice, holy, acceptable unto God, which is your reasonable service" (Romans 12:1).

Fire is an indication of the power and energy of God. "For the Lord thy God is a consuming fire" (Deuteronomy 4:24). "Understand therefore this day, that the Lord thy God is he which goeth before thee; as a consuming fire he shall destroy them, and he shall bring them down before thy face: so shalt thou drive them out, and destroy them quickly, as the Lord hath said unto thee" (Deuteronomy 9:3).

How often we learn the hard way that it is impossible to overcome our enemies and obstacles without the help of the Lord! And how many times do we have to be assured and reassured that our God is a consuming fire and that He will go before us to face the giants of sin and opposition? "Wherefore we receiving a kingdom which cannot be moved, let us have grace, whereby we may serve God acceptably with reverence and godly fear: For our God is a consuming fire" (Hebrews 12:28, 29).

Fire is a refiner, a revealer and a renovator. The Bible refers to the presence of Christ the Messiah saying, "He is like a refiner's fire, and like fullers' soap" (Malachi 3:2). The *Living Bible* paraphrases the full context, " 'He is like a blazing fire refining precious metal and he can bleach the dirtiest garments! Like a refiner of silver he will sit and closely watch as the dross is burned away. He will purify the Levites, the ministers of God, refining them like gold or silver, so that they will do their work for God with pure hearts.' "

Man's work is revealed and made manifest as by fire. He is also saved as by fire (1 Corinthians 3:13-15). The renovation of the whole earth by the fire of God's judgment is mentioned in 2 Peter 3:7, 10-13. Verse 11 applies its truth in these terms, "Seeing then that all these things shall be dissolved, what manner of persons ought ye to be in all holy conversation and godliness." The true child of God should not fear the fire of the Lord but rather welcome its purifying and preserving quality. Beware, however, of the type of strange fire and false fire spoken of in connection with Nadab and Abihu in Leviticus 10:1, 2 and Numbers 3:4; 26:61. God will not abide sacrilege, chicanery, self-exaltation, pride, obstinance and deception in the place and performance of His holy worship.

"Who maketh his ministers a flaming fire" (Psalm 104:4). God's representatives are so full of sanctified zeal and the Spirit's anointing that nothing which hell affords can stand against them. They are like Jesus of whom it is written, "The zeal of thine house hath eaten me up" (Psalm 69:9; John 2:17). All other desires and passions have been consumed and swallowed up by the one desire for the things of God.

The root meaning of the word *fervent* suggests heat, energy, very hot, glowing, burning, boiling, zealous, ardent, warm in feelings and devotion, intensity, fiery, shining, eager, flaming, impassioned, intent yet without violence. It flows with natural intensity from the individual, and glows without bursting into flame. Now that is getting mighty hot, isn't it? It is warm, spontaneous and filled with enthusiasm which suggests energy, strength and spon-taneity. On and on the fervor of a heart in communication with the heavenly Father mounts and escalates higher and higher.

Divinity and humanity, the Creator and His creation, come together in understanding, reasoning, petition, in-spiration, need and in holy communication. God by His Spirit is communicating with man; and man by the same Spirit is communicating with God. It all reminds me of the home missionary visiting a small congregation in a poverty-stricken area of the mountains. They drove as far as they could and then hiked up a trail for a short distance. When they arrived for service, the small building was packed. It was illuminated only by lanterns, and there were no musical instruments except a washboard and some homemade utensils. They were all standing, clapping their hands and singing, "God's got a fire—He don't need no matches!"

How to Pray With a Fervent Spirit

When Helen and I went to pastor the Meridian Street Church in Nashville, my first message on Sunday morning was from Romans 12. It seems I preached every Sunday morning for about six months from Romans 12. It was as though I had taken hold of something that I couldn't turn loose. It is a wonderful and practical passage: "Not slothful in business; fervent in spirit; serving the Lord" (v. 11).

It means a person should never be lazy, slow or careless in the work of the Lord. In other words, he gives God's work and God's business top priority, maintaining zeal to the boiling point, putting his life into service for God whether or not he receives personal gain or applause. He does so with a fervency and vigor that is divine. His very breath, wind, thrust, drive and the chemistry of his being is aglow with the fire of the Holy Spirit, and he does everything with maximum energy and power. And little wonder—he is doing the work and the will of Almighty God!

We have an example of this in Acts 18:25, "This man [Apollos] was instructed in the way of the Lord; and being fervent in the spirit, he spake and taught diligently the things of the Lord, knowing only the baptism of John." Having had an illustrious background, Apollos was in many ways similar to Paul. He grew up in the city of Alexandria. Alexander the Great had built the city during the peak of the Grecian Renaissance. Some of the great universities and one of the seven wonders of the world were located there. In fact, it is said the Septuagint was translated in their universities. The Septuagint is the translation of the Old Testament Hebrew Scriptures into the Greek language. It marked the bringing together of two great cultures.

Apollos was a product of these universities. He had only tasted of the good things of God. He was zealous and set on fire. He wanted to take the knowledge and the skills he had acquired and apply them immediately to the work of the Lord.

The Living Bible paraphrases,

> *After spending some time there, he [Paul] left for Turkey again through Galatia and Phrygia visiting all the believers, encouraging them and helping them to grow in the Lord. As it happened, a Jew named Apollos, a wonderful Bible teacher and preacher, had just arrived in Ephesus from Alexandria in Egypt. While he was in Egypt, someone had told him about John the Baptist and what John said about Jesus, but that is all he knew. He had never heard the rest of the story! So he was preaching boldly and enthusiastically in the synagogues. 'The Messiah is coming,' he said. 'Get ready to receive Him.' Priscilla and Aquilla were there and heard him—and it was a powerful sermon. Afterwards they met with him and explained what had happened to Jesus since the time of John and all that it meant. Apollos had been thinking about going to Greece, and the believers encouraged him in this. They wrote their fellow believers there, telling them to welcome him. And upon his arrival in Greece, he was greatly used of God to strengthen the church, for he powerfully reputed all the Jewish arguments in public debate, showing by the Scriptures that Jesus is indeed the Messiah (Acts 18:23-28).*

Here is a man that was full of zeal and fire, determined to be involved in the work of the Lord. Aquilla and

Priscilla, sitting back in the congregation, knew that he had been shortchanged somewhere along the line, and they agreed to help him.

Many times we have seen individuals get that first taste of the Spirit's fire, a little appetizer of the good things of God, and they want to jump right in the middle of everything and become an authority overnight.

Some years ago many of the people who grew up in Pentecostalism and were founders of some of the oldest churches had written little about this. Then overnight someone would come along who had just received the baptism of the Holy Spirit a few weeks or months prior and would put out a book as an authority on receiving the Baptism—as an authority on the Pentecostal experience. This was similar to what happened to Apollos. He received a little taste and became so excited that he was right in the middle of things before he knew it.

Some of Paul's coworkers who were solidly founded in the Word said, "This enthusiasm is good; let's help him." They didn't criticize him. They simply went to him, took him by the hand and took him into their hearts with love and understanding. The King James Version says, "They . . . expounded unto him the way of God more perfectly" (Acts 18:26).

How often we see fire, fervor and enthusiasm and want to pour cold water on it. What we need to do is appreciate the fire and the fervor and, if it needs a little help, use some patience, longsuffering and wisdom to give it guidance— but let the fire burn! It's hard to put fire in them, but once they have it, get it under control and things will begin to happen.

I praise God for the fire and the enthusiasm of Christian workers. I also praise God for His truth. And I'm glad that the fire and the fervor can be wrapped up in truth and

119

authority that will help us reach others for Jesus Christ and accomplish His work.

Apollos' energies, his burning desire and flaming spirit, were placed in the strength and cloak of the Word, and as a result, he was a great blessing and help to the church. *Lord, teach us to pray fervently! Teach us to pray with a fervent spirit for the things of God.*

How to Pray With a Fervent Mind

"He [Titus] told us your earnest desire, your mourning, your fervent mind toward me; so that I rejoiced the more" (2 Corinthians 7:7). Paul had problems in one of his churches. It became his responsibility to write them a very stern letter. Paul, being the spiritual leader and human being that he was, naturally was apprehensive about the strong letter he had to write to the people he loved so dearly. He knew if his letter didn't help them, things would get worse rather than get better. Therefore, shouldering his responsibility, which can be painful, he wrote the letter, wondering how they were going to take it and how they were going to respond.

You can imagine the time involved in sending a letter and waiting for word to come back. Paul actually wondered if he should have sent the letter. Maybe he should have watered it down a little. All those questions kept coming to his mind. Finally, Titus arrived and told him, "Paul, I want to give you a report, and it's going to be a good report." He began to tell him about the services, how the Spirit of God melted their hearts. He told him about the letter, that it was hard and that it cut, but it was disciplinary action that was needed. Titus said, "Rather than the people rebelling and fighting back, they began to weep and repent and ask forgiveness. They were not only sorry for their problem and for the things that had gotten out of control, they were also sorry because you were hurt and had to take action that would cause you to feel pain because they knew how much you loved them."

When Paul heard Titus, he wrote the people and said, "Titus told me of your earnestness, of your brokenness, and of your fervent mind toward me." The divine fire of the Holy Spirit will not only burn up the negatives, it will refine and purify the positives with the glow of God's holiness.

I'm glad that our emotions and our spirits can be on fire. I'm glad that our mentality, intellect, thought process and reasoning can also be anointed with the same fire. The idea that fire only gets in the feet, the hands and the heart is erroneous. The fire of God and the fervency of the Spirit covers the totality of man, including his intellect.

Lord, when You teach us to pray, show us that we should not only pray enthusiastically and emotionally, but intellectually as well. Teach us that the fire and fervency of God can quicken our mental faculties as well as the rest of our being. Lord, teach us to pray with a fervent mind!

Prayer is still rational, even though it sometimes pursues the impossible. Someone has asked just how rational prayer is. It is just as rational as the Word of God. Praise God, we can pray with a fervent spirit and a fervent mind.

How to Pray With a Fervent Love

"See that ye love one another with a pure heart fervently" (1 Peter 1:22). "The end of all things is at hand: be ye therefore sober, and watch unto prayer. And above all things have fervent charity among yourselves: for charity shall cover the multitude of sins" (1 Peter 4:7, 8).

In *The Living Bible* 1 Peter 1:22 reads, "Now you can have real love for everyone because your souls have been cleansed from selfishness and hatred when you trusted

Christ to save you; so see to it that you really do love each other warmly, with all your hearts." And 1 Peter 4:7, 8 reads, "The end of the world is coming soon. Therefore be earnest, thoughtful men of prayer. Most important of all, continue to show deep love for each other, for love makes up for many of your faults."

Prayer must be a primary factor in the development of genuine, qualitative love relationships. Many so-called friendships have little or no basis for longevity or survival.

Paul was saying, let your love be earnest, zealous, abundant, fervent and unceasing. It is not that love will cause God to look past sins and faults. No! It is a love that will help us to look past imperfections in others and not hold grudges. Do nothing merely because it is commanded, but rather do it because of your love for God and man. "The love of Christ constraineth us" (2 Corinthians 5:14). It presses us, pushes and overpowers us until we have no other choice. As Paul Henson puts it, "I can't help it; I can't do anything about it; I can't help but love you. It is the love of Christ that compels me to do so." *Lord, teach us to pray with a fervent love!*

How to Pray Fervent Prayers

"Epaphras, who is one of you, a servant of Christ, saluteth you, always labouring fervently for you in prayers, that ye may stand perfect and complete in all the will of God. For I bear him record, that he hath a great zeal for you" (Colossians 4:12, 13).

Epaphras was a fellow worker with Paul and a fellow prisoner in Rome. Paul really knew him. He told the people, "He is always praying for you, asking God to make you strong, to make you perfect and to help you to know His will. He is zealous for you. He works hard in your behalf." Helen and I would have never made it this far had it not been for the many who have labored fervently for us in prayer. Many have been the letters and calls which have come to us saying, "On a certain date at a certain time we were impressed to pray for you." Paul said he could vouch for his friend and colleague. Epaphras had a deep interest and a real passion for their welfare.

It is one thing to say a prayer and it is another thing to pray a prayer. I still love that old song which says,

> Pray till your prayers go through,
> Pray till your prayers go through.
> It will give you gladness,
> Take away your sadness,
> If you'll pray till your prayers go through.
> —B.C. Robinson

Lord, teach us to pray with a fervent spirit, a fervent mind, a fervent love, and especially to pray fervent prayers.

Prayer

Thank You, our Father, for the fire of life, love and liberty which You bring into our lives. Purge us with hyssop that we may be clean. Burn out all the dross and impurities that we might be refined and fashioned in Your image. Grant us a fervency that only Your Holy Spirit can give. This we pray in Jesus' name. Amen.

CHAPTER
—10—

PRAYING
EARNESTLY

Years ago there were two men who had a radio talk show. I'm not sure if they adapted it for television or not, but I well remember the name of the program—*Frank and Earnest*, the first names of the two gentlemen. They dealt with pertinent questions brought to them through the mail or by telephone. Undoubtedly, it was characteristic of them to answer questions frankly and to deal with inquiries earnestly. Perhaps this example illustrates the title of this chapter, "How to Pray Earnestly." The text is Luke 22:44: "And being in an agony he prayed more earnestly: and his sweat was as it were great drops of blood falling down to the ground."

When the word *earnest* is used in the Scriptures as a noun, it means "to pledge." When it is used as an adverb or an adjective, it means "to be eager, sincere and serious." It would therefore be very much in order for us to just say, "Lord, teach us to pray eagerly, sincerely and seriously. Lord, teach us to pray earnestly!" "Then an angel from heaven appeared and strengthened him, for he was in such agony of spirit that he broke into a sweat of blood, with great drops falling to the ground as he prayed more and more earnestly" (Luke 22:44, *TLB*).

Notice four things from this particular passage of

Scripture. (1) Jesus prayed, (2) He prayed more, (3) He prayed earnestly, and (4) He prayed more earnestly.

Jesus Prayed

The first and most important part of this passage is the fact that *Jesus prayed*.

The Background

There is definitely a background which precipitated this action of prayer. Judas had already agreed to betray Jesus. Preparations and arrangements had been made for Jesus to keep the Passover with His disciples. It would be His last meal with those He loved before His crucifixion. Thus, He instituted the Last Supper, which we know as the Lord's Supper. Many of us still observe this occasion each Lord's Day, the first Sunday of the month or at other special times in remembrance of our Lord.

Jesus had foretold during the supper that He would be betrayed by one of His very own. There was also strife among the group. The discussion was "Who will be the greatest in the Kingdom?" (Luke 22:24). Can you imagine how this sounded to Jesus? In a matter of hours He would be crucified. He would die for the sins of the world. But now He was listening to the things occupying the minds of His closest followers. Who would be first in the Kingdom? Who would sit on the right hand and who would sit on the left? Peter's denial was also foretold. Jesus then did something that He had often done. He led them out to the Mount of Olives.

The Agony

Verse 44 begins, "And being in agony He prayed." This word *agony* is from the word *agonia*, which means "a

126

struggle" or "a conflict." It means more than just physical pain, physical struggle and physical conflict. With whom then did He struggle? The Bible answers in 1 Peter 5:8, "Your adversary the devil, as a roaring lion, walketh about, seeking whom he may devour." "For we wrestle not against flesh and blood, but against principalities, against powers, against the rulers of the darkness of this world, against spiritual wickedness in high places" (Ephesians 6:12).

Jesus was aware that He was in a conflict, a struggle, a battle. He was aware that all conflicts and struggles come from one source. That source is the diabolical one whose name is *Diabolos*, meaning one with a diabolical character and personality—one who loves to antagonize, to destroy, to come against you, to cause conflict, problems and trouble. That one is the devil himself who was out to sabotage the plan of redemption, to wreck the plan of salvation. He is still trying to stop the thrust of the Great Commission and to discredit the church of the living God.

Jesus prayed. His life was one of conflict. He faced the common struggles that we all face. We need to take care lest we begin to think we have attained, we have arrived, that there is no more enemy, conflict, warfare or struggle, and that life at last is a bed of roses and Pentecost is a perpetual picnic. If we think life is a picnic, we had better look again! This life is a warfare; this life is a battlefield. If the divine Son of God encountered such problems, rest assured His body, the church of the living God, is still engaged in the same warfare. Whenever we meet the same problems Jesus encountered, we too must pray as Jesus prayed. The Bible says, "Being in agony, He prayed."

With whom was the conflict and opposition? You will observe that Christ had opposition from without and opposition from within. Not only was He opposed by Satan, He was also opposed by many others. The Bible says, "He came unto His own, and His own received Him not" (John 1:4). Jesus was opposed by the Jews—His own people and His own race. The things He proposed were counter also to the Caesar and the Roman government who was in power at that time. He was in conflict with the chief priest, religious leaders and Pontius Pilate, the governor. He was in conflict with Caiphas, the high priest. He was in conflict with the elders. Many were the outside opposers of Christ. His opposition was definitely external.

He faced conflict and opposition from within as well. He chose 12, and one of them was openly, deliberately and premeditatively against Him. Judas betrayed Him and sold Him for 30 pieces of silver. Even Peter, who was to be the chief pillar of His church, cursed and denied Him after vowing that he would never do so. Two out of 12, some might say, is not a bad percentage. In the final analysis, however, the Bible says, "They all forsook Him and fled" (Mark 14:50). Conflict—struggle—opposition from without—opposition from within. "Being in agony, He prayed" (Luke 22:44).

Jesus Prayed More

Prayer Helps Us to Overcome Opposition

The Bible also says, "He prayed more" (Luke 22:44). Every time you read this verse it seems to build in intensity. One time alone is not enough. You need to read it and reread it, again and again. "And being in agony, He prayed more" (Luke 22:44). The opposition that Jesus encountered was real. Such opposition must always be overcome. It was either Christ or Caesar, Jesus or Judas, sin or salvation. "For this purpose the Son of God was manifested, that he might destroy the works of the devil" (1 John 3:8). Christ came to destroy the works of Satan and give the believer complete mastery over them. He came to put down rebellion, the works of darkness, moral seduction and sexual perversion. He came to change the wicked heart of man and give him a *new* heart like unto the heart of God.

Prayer Helps Us to Attain Our Goals

Jesus was not only overcoming opposition, He was also attaining a goal. Christ was on assignment. He had a mission to accomplish. His task was given to Him by His heavenly Father. All eternity and all of the family of mankind was depending on Him. The whole plan of God was at stake. The Bible says the reason for His coming was to "save His people from their sins" (Matthew 1:21). He came to be a sacrifice for sins once and for all (Hebrews 9:28). He came that we might have life and that we might have it more abundantly (John 10:10). Jesus was that "gift of God" sent down from heaven to cancel man's penalty of death and provide for all "eternal life" (Romans 6:23). As Kenneth Taylor paraphrases, "He prayed more and more" (*TLB*). When the battle became tougher, Jesus went further and prayed harder. When the conflict intensified, so did His spirit and His prayers.

He had a goal, a task and a mission. He was on assignment. What was that goal? Whatever it was, He accomplished it! Redemption was assured for all believers. The plan of salvation was set in motion! He laid the foundation for it, gave it impetus, credibility, authority, and turned the mission over to us to finish the unfinished task. You and I are in the same warfare, the same struggle, the same conflict. We are facing the same opposition that Jesus faced.

The Mission of the Church

What, then, is the goal and mission of the church? Why

does the church exist? First of all, the mission of the church is to seek and to save the lost. This is primary; this must be number one in the hearts and minds of believers. The Great Commission is parallel to Christ's mission. Jesus said in John 20:21, "As my Father hath sent me, *even so* send I you." Our task is the unfinished task! Our mission is to complete, carry out and finish that which He began. The church is to go and make disciples of all men, in all nations throughout the world. Every action, song, sermon or plan of every member, minister and friend must be contributing to that eternal quest which is the heartbeat of God—the salvation of lost souls. This is why we exist; it is our reason for being on planet Earth.

Those who are saved must be discipled in order to duplicate themselves by winning others so the cycle never ends. The action of winning the lost never stops; it goes on and on. The goal Jesus had on this earth, the plan Satan tried to sabotage, is still the same—it has not changed. If Jesus "being in agony prayed," and being in agony "prayed more," likewise the church today will need to pray and will need to pray more.

Jesus Prayed Earnestly

The word *earnest* is used sparingly in both the Old Testament and the New Testament. When it is used to describe praying, it does not refer to ordinary praying. It means extraordinary praying. It means more than a formal memorized prayer. It means more than a "Now I lay me down to sleep," recited-from-memory prayer. It speaks of extraordinary measures—called in to handle extraordinary circumstances. Most generally the measures taken are more than equal to circumstances.

Extraordinary Circumstances Require Extraordinary Praying

Extraordinary circumstances are prevalent in this 20th century—the world is encountering situations never before faced in the history of man. Our nation is continually confronting crises and our communities are experiencing unbelievably abnormal conditions. The church is a part of that same world, nation and community. Our time calls for extraordinary praying. *Lord, teach us to pray earnestly!*

Ask yourself if the world has ever faced a global phenomenon comparable to the AIDS epidemic. We must pray not only for a cure for this disease, we must pray also for a revival that will change the lifestyle of those causing and spreading such a disease. This will require earnest praying, the kind of praying which is serious, sincere and means business. To pray for a cure alone without attacking the cause is ineffectual. Any effort toward finding a cure that ignores the cause and gives license for the flagrant abuse of the laws of God, the laws of man and the laws of nature will only accelerate a global bacterial armageddon. The only real cure for such a malady must of necessity deal with the cause.

Ask yourself if the world has ever faced a phenomenon comparable to the greenhouse effect, a thermonuclear holocaust and the chemical addiction of man's total genetic code. These are extraordinary times in which extraordinary men and women must pray extraordinary prayers and take extraordinary action if the human race is to survive.

Earnest Praying Is Eager, Sincere and Serious Praying

To be *eager* denotes "haste, forwardness, zeal and action." It means to be "ardent, burning and desirous." It is the opposite of dull, slow, passive and indifferent. When Jesus' parents went searching for Him when as a young adolescent He became lost in the crowd, they found Him in

131

the temple in the midst of doctors discussing the sacred Scriptures. His parents expressed concern. Jesus responded, "Wist ye not that I must be about my Father's business?" (Luke 2:49). He could wait no longer; the hour would not permit it. His time was so short. He had to get on with the task at hand.

Paul said to young Timothy, "Be instant in season, [and] out of season" (2 Timothy 4:2). Again he said, "Watch ye, stand fast in the faith, quit ye like men, be strong" (1 Corinthians 16:13). Earnest praying is aggressive praying. It is always in season. Earnest praying comes from a prepared intercessor who has "put on the whole armour of God, that . . . [he] may be able to stand against the wiles of the devil" (Ephesians 6:11).

Earnest praying is *sincere* praying—pure, true and real; it is a quality possessed by God because it is right, incorruptible, guileless and without hypocrisy. Its motives and goals are pure, scriptural and godly. Elijah "was a man subject to like passions as we are, and he prayed earnestly" (James 5:17). Elijah's circumstances demanded unquestionable sincerity. His prayer to God that it rain not was an answered prayer. "And he prayed again, and the heaven gave rain" (v. 18). He prayed! He prayed more! He prayed earnestly! It's time for the Christian church to get sincere with God. It's time for each of us as individuals to get in earnest with God. Rest assured that God has certainly been frank and earnest with us. Search the pages of world history and see if God has beat around the bush and been mealy-mouthed with the inhabitants of this planet. From the beginning God has been sincere with us. Now He wants us to be sincere with Him.

Earnest praying is also *serious* praying. It means to be "careful, diligent and to mean business." It has nothing whatsoever to do with lightness, jesting, manipulation or game playing. It is totally concerned with weighty, thoughtful, grave, sober matters of the highest importance. Christ's prayer in the Garden of Gethsemane was a matter of life and death for Him and for the world. Elijah's prayer on Mount Carmel was a matter of life and death for him and for the nation. Oh, what a difference it would make if we only realized that most of our praying has to do with life-and-death matters!

Listen to the seriousness of the Scriptures. "Wherefore lift up thy prayer for the remnant that are left" (2 Kings 19:4). "Except the Lord of hosts had left unto us a very small remnant, we should have been as Sodom, and we should have been like unto Gomorrah" (Isaiah 1:9).

Our prayers today should be equally as serious as Abraham's were for Lot in Sodom (Genesis 18:24-32) and as Moses' were about Israel's idolatry at Sinai (Exodus 32:30). Earnest prayer is the fruit of brotherly love, kindness and charity. When you love the church and the people of God as Jesus loved Jerusalem, you will pray for them. When you love your enemies and them that despitefully use you, you will pray for them. A centurion, who loved and genuinely cared for his servant, sought Christ and asked Him to speak the word of healing in his servant's behalf. "His servant was healed in the selfsame hour" (Matthew 8:13).

Earnestness in love will cause us to seek not our own things so much as the welfare of others. Any Jonathan who loves David will be a petitioner to his Father for him. Any queen, such as Esther, who loves her people will beg the king not only for her life but the lives of the nation also. As Abraham, Moses and Esther pled for their people, even so, the church must continually pray for the people and be appalled at the loss of even one. Like the good shepherd who hazarded his life for the one lost sheep, we too are in a life-and-death struggle. God's business is serious business.

How Many Times Do We Organize Rather Than Agonize?

Someone has said, "Anything but another committee!" (Is it true that the camel is a horse which a committee designed?) When I say *organize*, I'm not downing organization. Indeed, God is a God of organization. The Scriptures are replete with support of organization. However, organization is not enough.

The devil loves to antagonize. I pray that God's people will never forget how to agonize. That's what Jesus did. He learned early how to agonize. When God's people get desperate, things miraculously begin to happen. Agony speaks of anguish, desperation, distress, struggle and pain. How often is the contemporary church of the Lord Jesus Christ caught up with the opposite of what the early church did. The Bible says, "Woe to them that are at ease in Zion" (Amos 6:1).

Listen to the parable of the rich fool who says to his soul, "Soul, thou has much goods laid up for many years; take thine ease, eat, drink, and be merry. But God said unto him, Thou fool, this night thy soul shall be required of thee" (Luke 12:19, 20). "For as soon as Zion travailed, she brought forth her children" (Isaiah 66:8). When Zion travails, sons and daughters shall be born into the kingdom of God.

There are no shortcuts to genuine New Testament evangelism. Revivals continue to be born after the labor pains of prayer. *Travail* still speaks of "effort, labor, stress, toil, work and the painfulness of a mother's birth pangs experienced during the delivery of her child." Paul says, "My little children, of whom I travail in birth again until Christ be formed in you" (Galatians 4:19). This is the second time Paul had labored in preaching, prayers, tears and soul travail until they were born into the family of God. Now again he refused to give them up to the

134

bewitching elements of the world (Galatians 3:1). This was the commitment of Paul, and this was the commitment of Christ. He prayed! He prayed more! And he prayed earnestly!

Jesus Prayed More Earnestly

The Pressure Never Lets Up

The pressure never lets up in the kingdom of God. We wonder sometimes why missionaries never take furloughs and ministers never take vacations. Helen and I took two days vacation in four years in Florida. I promised my children when we went to the Dakotas we would see the country. We had pastored there in the early '50s and hadn't really seen any of the country. I told our son and daughter, Steve and Rene, "We'll see the country this time." We were suddenly in our fourth and final year. Steve came in one day, as he was now a teenager, saying, "Well, Dad, we're about to leave. We're going to the General Assembly. You've already gotten your letter from the general overseer saying you won't be back. We've been out here four years, and we haven't seen anything yet."

I got the message. We loaded the car and left in a matter of hours and saw three national parks on the way to the General Assembly. The pressure never lets up! There is no way you can get away from it.

The pressure on Jesus was indeed uncommon, and it continued to mount. Christ saw what was happening. It was the compulsion of a great compassion! It was a life-and-death struggle, and the intensity was growing. May God forgive the mockery of those who play games with Him and the church. We need to be told again and again, "This is not a game, this is God!" This is for real—the only reality! The rest is tinsel and tinfoil and will be burned as chaff.

Luke the Physician Wrote This Passage

Of all the people who could write this particular passage, it had to be Luke the physician. No other writer could describe this particular incident in the terms he selected. He used medical terms. Listen to the words: *agony, drops of blood, sweat, more earnestly, falling all the way to the ground.*

The root of *agony* was *agon*, meaning "the area or arena for assembling a contest, where the participants encountered one another." You either won or lost; and if you lost, you died. In this particular case Jesus died, but He won because He triumphed over all His foes. That's the kind of conflict and contest the Christian encounters today. The word *drops* means "gouts or clots of blood." *Sweat* refers to that which accompanies agony. *Blood* is mentioned in medical history where the pores of the skin dilate under extreme mental pressure until actual blood oozes or issues from the pores of the skin and it becomes a *bloody sweat.*

Did you ever wonder who Luke's informants were? Where did he get this information? It could have been the soldiers casting lots for His garments. Did they observe the stains on His tunic? It could have been Mary Magdalene who stood by the cross at His crucifixion. She could have noticed it. Or it could have been Nicodemus or Joseph of Aramathea when they embalmed His body. They could have noticed and reported it to Luke. It was an exceptional circumstance, one which necessitated Luke's recording. He prayed, He prayed more, and He prayed more earnestly.

When James 5:17 speaks of Elijah as "a man subject to like passions as we are, and *he prayed earnestly*," it gives us the right, the permission and the opportunity to do likewise. *Lord, teach us to pray earnestly!*

Since Helen and I have been in the ministry, we have conducted many funerals. I am not a medical person, but if I were, I think I would do a little research concerning missionaries, evangelists, pastors and Christian workers who meet untimely deaths. I would like to know and have some actual professional understanding of the physical stresses and pressures on their hearts.

My mind goes immediately to the time one of our leaders suffered an untimely death. The doctors said his heart "exploded." Then one of our World Missions directors barely survived a severe seizure. He was a man small in stature. They said the little physical muscle called a heart had such pressure on it that it just came apart. The doctors had a hard time getting it back together. I ministered to one of our pastors in Florida who had a successful career. He had been at one church for many years and had done a great work in the inner city. He and his family had truly ministered to this downtown congregation. After his death, the doctor told the family and me that the bottom of his heart just fell out.

If the story of the bleeding hearts of the Christian world could be told, I wonder how many would have experienced similar agony to that which Jesus experienced? He prayed more, He prayed earnestly, and He prayed more earnestly.

I have personally visited one of the largest, fastest growing churches in the world. When they meet for worship, they first of all go to prayer. They pray so fervently and so earnestly it is necessary to set a clock. The clock has a bell on it, and the pastor has to ring the bell to stop them. If the pastor doesn't ring the bell, they pray on and on. Prayer meetings are held on the grounds 24 hours a day. When the church has problems, solutions are always found in prayer. Wherever there is a lack of prayer, a lack of fervency, earnestness and results, there is a spiritual problem.

In general, if a church has financial problems, it can be traced to spiritual problems. Almost any kind of problem encountered in the kingdom of God can be traced right back to spiritual problems. The way to solve spiritual problems is by the Word of God, on our face and on our knees, following the example of the Lord Jesus Christ. He prayed, He prayed more, He prayed earnestly, and He prayed more earnestly. *Lord, teach us to pray!*

Compare verses 44 and 45 in Luke 22. "And when he [Jesus] rose up from prayer, and was come to his disciples, he found them sleeping" (v. 45).

Prayer

Our Father, we thank You for Your presence and for Your Word. It is a Word that does not always give us what we want, but we can rest assured that it always gives us what we need. Thank You for the church, for every member, friend, family, department and agency of truth and service. May Your special graces be upon each of them. We pray that You will make the church of the Lord Jesus Christ fruitful. Use us all in the salvation of lost souls, to lift up the hands of our leaders, to minister to the body of Christ and to hasten the completion of the Great Commission. This we pray in Jesus' name. Amen.

CHAPTER

—— 11 ——

PRAYING
MEDITATIVELY

The history of the church's progress is usually the history of its prayer life. Few things happen in the Kingdom that are not accredited to the power of prayer. If prayer does not drive sin out of our lives, then sin will drive prayer out of our lives. One or the other will prevail. One or the other will have to go. Prayer does not need proof; it only needs practice. Prayer is not to ask what we wish of God but rather what God wishes of us. When we truly pray, we will surrender to Him so that He has primary place in our lives. This is why the psalmist prayed in Psalm 19:14, "Let the words of my mouth, and the meditation of my heart, be acceptable in thy sight, O Lord, my strength, and my redeemer."

A motto hanging on a church wall says, "If you must whisper, whisper a prayer." We are so accustomed to the enthusiasm of worship that we forget the Lord can also communicate in a still small voice. He is not only in the whirlwind, He is also in the gentle breeze. When we get into a state of panic or a crisis, our volume and intensity is sometimes determined by the depth of the emergency. Why does it seem that most of our time spent with God is during the storm and stress rather than the quiet and rest of life? God is for all time, not just part-time. We need to take time to contemplate and think about God.

The Mind and Its Meditation

The word *meditate* means "to think, ponder, muse, reflect, dwell in deep thought and reflection." When we can think through a matter, it seems to clear everything else out of the way and allow us to have more purity of thought. This permits the traffic of our mind to be unincumbered, uncrowded, unhurried and unrushed.

Elton Trueblood once said, "Ours is a cut-flower society," meaning "we have no roots." I think our prayer life suffers from the same malady. It is often groundless and pointless. If only we would spend time in meditation and con-templation, then our reasoning and our supplication might have more depth. Many of our prayers do not have the character and the meaning they ought to have. Oh, that the Great Intercessor in heaven, now seated at the right hand of the Father, might teach us by His Word how to pray meditatively after contemplating, musing and dwelling in the secret place of the most high and abiding under the shadow of the Almighty (Psalm 91:1).

Let us begin by considering Psalm 8:3-9:

> *When I consider thy heavens, the work of thy fingers, the moon and the stars, which thou hast ordained; What is man, that thou art mindful of him? and the son of man, that thou visitest him? For thou hast made him a little lower than the angels, and hast crowned him with glory and honour. Thou madest him to have dominion over the works of thy hands; thou has put all things under his feet: All sheep and oxen, yea, and the beasts of the field; The fowl of the air, and the fish of the sea, and whatsoever passeth through the paths of the seas. O Lord our Lord, how excellent is thy name in all the earth!*

David was saying in these verses, "When I look up into the night skies and see the work of Your fingers, the moon and the stars that You have made, I cannot understand how You can bother with man. You have made him only a little lower than the angels and placed a crown of glory and honor upon his head. You have put him in charge of everything You have made. Everything is put under his authority; all sheep and oxen, wild animals, birds, fish, and all the life of the sea. O Jehovah, our Lord, the majesty and glory of Your name fills all the earth."

David was simply contemplating and thinking about God; not necessarily in the daytime, because if he were thinking of Him only in the daytime, he would see Him in that huge ball of fire roaming around heaven all day. But at this particular time, he was seeing the moon and the stars. "And when I consider the heavens and the work of Your hands, I am made to ask what is man—minute, finite man—that thou art mindful of him?"

Someone said there are over a million suns the size of our sun in our galaxy alone. If this is true, can you imagine the mind of man probing all of God's great big heaven and then finally asking what is man that God is so mindful of him? What is man that the actions of the ages, the supreme act of God in history, centers around this one finite being? What is it about man that allowed him, of all creatures, to be made in the image and likeness of God?

David in Psalm 8 and other psalms said in essence, "When I contemplate this, when I think about this and understand who You are, the infinite sovereign, omnipotent God, and realize also who man is, though finite, yet crowned with glory and honor and authority above all things, it consumes my thought patterns and impacts my worship and my prayers." The quality of our thinking will directly affect the quality of our praying.

David mused and contemplated not only at night but also in the daytime. His understanding of God's place and God's position in all of the universe didn't change. He said,

> *The heavens are telling the glory of God; they are a marvelous display of his craftsmanship. Day and night they keep on telling about God. Without a sound or word, silent in the skies, their message reaches out to all the world. The sun lives in the heavens where God placed it and moves out across the skies as radiant as a bridegroom going to his wedding, or as joyous as an athlete looking forward to a race! The sun crosses the heavens from end to end, and nothing can hide from its heat* (Psalm 19:1-6, *TLB*).

In Proverbs 6:6-10 David cautions, "Take a lesson from the ants, you lazy fellow. Learn from their ways to be wise! For though they have no king to make them work, yet they labor hard all summer, gathering food for the winter. But you—all you do is sleep. When will you wake up? . . . As you sleep, poverty creeps upon you like a robber and destroys you; want attacks you in full armor" (Proverbs 6:6-11, *TLB*).

Then he goes on,

> *Let me describe for you a . . . wicked man; first, he is a constant liar; he signals his true intentions to his friends with eyes and feet and fingers. Next, his heart is full of rebellion. And he spends his time thinking of all the evil he can do, and stirring up discontent. But he will be destroyed suddenly, broken beyond hope of healing. For these are six things the Lord hates—no, seven: haughtiness, lying, murdering, plotting evil, eagerness to do wrong, a false witness, sewing discord among brothers* (Proverbs 6:12-19, *TLB*).

He is really telling us to learn lessons from the small and simple things that we see in our world every day by looking around, perceiving and understanding. This can help to strengthen our prayer life and build it upon a solid foundation, surrounded by a super structure that will enable us to endure the test of time.

Jesus calls us to "consider the lilies of the field, how they grow; they toil not, neither do they spin: and yet I say unto you, That even Solomon in all his glory was not arrayed like one of these. Wherefore, if God so clothe the grass of the field, which to day is, and to morrow is cast into the oven, shall he not much more clothe you, O ye of little faith?" (Matthew 6:28-30).

Before we pray, we ought to think. Every time we pray, part of our prayer ought to be the concentration of our minds upon God, the Word of God and the things of God. Our minds should not be cluttered with the trappings of everything else, but rather truth should reign in our minds. His truth should be our guide and counselor, our shield and buckler as we put on the garments of praise for our approach into the presence of our heavenly Father.

"Consider the ravens: for they neither sow nor reap; which neither have storehouse nor barn; and God feedeth them: how much more are ye better than the fowls?" (Luke 12:24). Seldom do we ever go to God in prayer unless we take out our list. We always seem to have a list of what we want and what we don't want. If we really understood how God cares for us, how He cares for all the universe, how He cares for all of nature, how He has planned and balanced nature, then our prayer list might be different.

Let Us Continue by Cleansing

When the psalmist said, "Let the words of my mouth, and the meditations of my heart, be acceptable in thy sight,

O Lord, my strength, and my redeemer" (Psalm 19:14), I believe he wanted us to take a new and meaningful look at the meditations of our heart and mind to make sure the things we house there are in the best interest of the proprietor.

During the days of hurt and sorrow after the untimely death of his son, Dr. Paul L. Walker said, "In the wee hours of the morning, I found myself searching for something to do. Suddenly I opened the door of the closet that I had been wanting to clean out for a long time. In the middle of the night, I would be in there cleaning out the closet, throwing things every which way because I needed something to do. It was therapeutic for me to be doing something, and this seemed to be the most profitable thing to do at the time."

It might be good for us to go through the closets of our minds and clean them out. I think we'd be surprised at the clutter which has accumulated over the years. We've been afraid to clean out the things that clog up the free flow of God's wisdom, truth and holiness. If the channels were open and clean, there would be room for something more useful and needful to reside there. Far too many are lounging in the complacency of past accomplishments, rather than seizing the challenge of present opportunities. Paul says in Philippians 3:13, 14, "This one thing I do, forgetting those things which are behind, and reaching forth unto those things which are before, I press toward the mark for the prize of the high calling of God in Christ Jesus."

"Set your affection on things above, not on things on the earth" (Colossians 3:2). "Thy word have I hid in mine heart, that I might not sin against thee" (Psalm 119:11). "Having therefore these promises, dearly beloved, let us cleanse ourselves from all filthiness of the flesh and spirit, perfecting holiness in the fear of God" (2 Corinthians 7:1). Wholesome thought processes and a proper mental attitude are important parts of our prayer life.

Not Only a Pure Mind But Also a Clean Heart

David prayed in Psalm 51:10, "Create in me a clean heart, O God; and renew a right spirit within me." In Luke 11:39 and Matthew 23:25, 27, the Pharisees emphasized the cleaning of the outside of the vessel, forgetting and overlooking the inside. They wanted to look pious and religious. If they didn't have anything on the inside, they tried to make up for it with a lot of pomp and circumstance. The Bible, however, tells us that the inside was full of dead men's bones like a graveyard (Matthew 23:27). Jesus urged in verse 26, "Cleanse first that which is within the cup and platter, that the outside of them may be clean also." Note, please, the most difficult group with which Jesus had to deal was the religious leaders of His day who supposedly knew it all and had all the answers. They were totally impervious and resistant to any instructions, advice, counsel or communication.

"But how can I ever know what sins are lurking in my heart? Cleanse me from these hidden faults. And keep me from deliberate wrongs; help me to stop doing them. Only then can I be free of guilt and innocent of some great crime. May my spoken words and unspoken thoughts be pleasing even to you, O Lord, my Rock and my Redeemer" (Psalm 19:12-14).

The action of God's cleansing and purifying power is generally evidenced in two ways: moving out and moving in. There is a cleaning out, a getting rid of the impurities so that one can have the purities move in. That's exactly what happens in sanctification when you are getting ready for the infilling of the Holy Spirit. Sanctification cleans out, gets rid of and makes room for the Holy Spirit to move in and take up His abode. There is a reason for the cleansing and the purifying process. Then, and only then, can we truly meditate as we ought upon God and the things of God.

How to Meditate as We Ought

Now that we have made preparation, let us proceed with instruction.

Meditation Often Entails Reflection

"I remember the days of old; I meditate on all thy works; I muse on the work of thy hands" (Psalm 143:5). Sometimes it does us good to look back and review the things of the past. There are certain things we like and other things we don't like. I think, however, that remembering and reminiscing is wholly scriptural. "They shall abundantly utter the memory of thy great goodness, and shall sing of thy righteousness" (Psalm 145:7). "The memory of the just is blessed" (Proverbs 10:7). "Keep in memory what I preached unto you" (1 Corinthians 15:2). David learned from the present and from the past. One writer said, "Use the past for a springboard, not as a sofa." Madam Chiang Kai-shek concluded, "We live in the present, we dream of the future, but we learn eternal truths from the past." Maria, the energetic young Austrian wife whose family escaped the Nazi occupation of her country in World War II, spoke of "remembering" as being one of her favorite things.

Meditation May Suggest Isolation—Getting Alone With Yourself and With God

"And Isaac went out to meditate in the field at the eventide: and he lifted up his eyes, and saw, and, behold, the camels were coming. And Rebekah lifted up her eyes, and when she saw Isaac, she lighted off the camel. For she had said unto the servant, What man is this that walketh in the field to meet us? And the servant had said, It is my master: therefore she took a vail, and covered herself" (Genesis 24:63, 64).

This is one of the many beautiful love stories found in the Bible. It seems to say many wonderful things happen to people who pray, who plan, who think, who pardon and who dream. The Hebrew word for *meditate* means to "bend down in body and mind." Isaac, no doubt, had many things on his mind. That's why he saw the need to take a walk out into the fields by himself that he might be able to spend time with his God in prayer, in deep thought and contemplation. It was from this stance, this divine vantage point, that the scene suddenly changes. In verse 67 Rebekah became Isaac's wife and was a great comfort to him throughout his life. This was a special union, one divinely ordered in many ways.

How often we mistakenly feel that God is only involved in salvation and healing with ministers and missionaries. How definitely all of us need to be aware that God is vitally involved in all major aspects of life. Isaac went out into the field to meditate. He needed some time alone with himself and with his God. It was there that he came face-to-face with Rebekah. It was a meeting that was no doubt supernaturally arranged in heaven because of praying parents, praying servants and praying young people.

Meditation May Even Include Education—The Study and Contemplation of Truth and Right
"I will meditate in thy precepts, and have respect unto thy ways. I will delight myself in thy statutes: I will not forget thy word" (Psalm 119:15, 16). "Mine eyes prevent

147

the night watches, that I might meditate in thy word" (v. 148). The Jews had four sections of three-hour watches, and the Romans had three sections of four-hour watches. David was saying, "Before the watchman proclaims the hour, I am already ahead of him. I am already awake, seeking God and meditating upon His Word. I lie awake throughout the night, that I might review His promises and renew my vows."

Many times in my travels with Dr. Ray H. Hughes I would awaken in the early hours of the morning to find his bed empty. He would be slumped on the floor where he had spent the night quietly in prayer.

In a revival meeting in Houston, Texas, I felt a special urge to spend the night in prayer. T.C. Messer was the pastor. I suggested to his wife, Ruth, that she slip me the key so I could go to the church to be by myself. However, the only way to get the key was to ask the pastor for it. When I asked, he inquired, "What are you going to do?" And I said, "Well, I would like to go to the church for a little while tonight." Discerning what I wanted to do, he responded, "Just a minute, and I'll join you!" There was no way Pastor Messer was going to let me pray all night long in Houston, Texas, without him. If anyone was going to be praying in his church, he was going to be there with them. He was often in prayer during the midnight watches. David said in Psalm 1:1, 2, "Blessed is the man that walketh not in the counsel of the ungodly, nor standeth in the way of sinners, nor sitteth in the seat of the scornful. But his delight is in the law of the Lord; and in his law doth he meditate day and night."

"This book of the law shall not depart out of thy mouth; but thou shalt meditate therein day and night, that thou mayest observe to do according to all that is written therein: for then thou shalt make thy way prosperous, and then thou shalt have good success" (Joshua 1:8).

"When I remember thee upon my bed, and meditate on thee in the night watches" (Psalm 63:6).

"I will meditate also of all thy work, and talk of thy doings" (Psalm 77:12).

"Meditate upon these things; give thyself wholly to them; that thy profiting may appear to all. Take heed unto thyself, and unto the doctrine; continue in them: for in doing this thou shalt both save thyself, and them that hear thee" (1 Timothy 4:15, 16).

The Importance of Meditation

"Be still, and know that I am God: I will be exalted among the heathen, I will be exalted in the earth" (Psalm 46:10). These words are a command of God, issued to bring about the ultimate purpose of God. How can we know? How can we come to grips with the eternal verities of life? Are they past finding out? Have we somehow bypassed them? Have they been forgotten forever with the passage of time? Or have they not yet come forth from the womb of time? The answer is, God can be known. He wants us to know Him in all His fullness. In order to do so, we will have to "be still."

Medical science would be the first to attest to man's hyperactivity. The whole world seems doomed to a destiny of more and more with less and less. It's the whole fabric of our existence. Our machines, gadgets and inventions are so designed. Now even genes are being manipulated. Plants and animals are bred so as to meet new hurry-up production standards. God says to the whole world, "If you want to know Me, you will have to slow down, even stop for a moment, and take time to look and listen to Me. "Be still, and know that I am God!" (Psalm 46:10).

We not only need to stop our hyperphysical activity, we need to rediscipline our emotional and mental pace. The command to "be still" not only means "to halt, stop, cease and desist," it also means to "be quiet and listen." An often overlooked yet vitally important part of prayer is the ability to listen. "O that ye would altogether hold your peace!" (Job 13:5). "Please be quiet," one version declares. A paraphrase could read, "If you should stop your vain talking altogether, it might prove that you are at last coming to your senses."

"Even a fool, when he holdeth his peace, is counted wise: and he that shutteth his lips is esteemed a man of understanding" (Proverbs 17:28).

Young Samuel's call from God came after he had retired to rest (1 Samuel 3:1-10). At first he mistook the voice of God for the voice of Eli. After the more experienced Eli, the priest, explained what was happening, Samuel returned to his rest. "And the Lord came, and stood, and called as at other times, Samuel, Samuel. Then Samuel answered, Speak; for thy servant heareth" (v. 10). Eli had wisely instructed the lad, "Go, lie down: and if shall be, if he call thee, that thou shalt say, Speak Lord, for thy servant heareth" (v. 9). There are times when all of us need to stop whatever we are doing and take time to look and listen for God.

Dr. Paul Yonggi Cho, pastor of the Yoido Full Gospel Church in Seoul, Korea, shared a testimony of how he was stricken in the early days of his ministry with a very serious heart attack. He was flat on his back, bedfast. He could not shave himself or even feed himself. He was almost totally helpless. He had worked so hard pastoring his growing church that his heart and body could go no further. One day while reading his Bible, he turned to the Twenty-third Psalm. The first phrase in verse two was as far as he could go. It appropriately reminded him, "He maketh me to lie down." Suddenly, reflecting on his helpless condition, Dr. Cho responded, "Lord, You certainly have made me to lie down. All I can do is to lie flat on my back and look up at the ceiling. I am totally helpless until You heal me and raise me up."

That is exactly what God did. He healed him and restored him brand new to his congregation, and he has been going ever since.

What will it take for God to get our attention? Will He have to resort to some natural phenomenon? Or will He have to again resort to the handwriting on the wall, the fire and brimstome of Sodom and Gomorrah, Noah's flood, a floating ax head, a talking donkey or a crowing rooster? God did everything imaginable to get Pharaoh's attention. Someone has suggested his head must have been as hard as his heart. Neither the preachers, the plagues nor the parting of the Red Sea slowed him down. God finally closed the sea up on both Pharaoh and his army. When God closes the book, rest assured it is closed forever. How simple and easy it would be for each of us to just "stand still and see the salvation of the Lord" (Exodus 14:13). Stand still and hear what Jehovah will command concerning you (Numbers 9:8). Stand still and consider the wondrous works of God (Job 37:14).

The hymn "Take Time to Be Holy" speaks clearly in verses one and two:

> Take time to be holy, Speak oft with Thy Lord;
> Abide in Him always, And feed on His Word:
> Make friends of God's children, Help those who are
>   weak;
> Forgetting in nothing His blessing to seek.
>
> Take time to be holy, The world rushes on;
> Spend much time in secret With Jesus alone:
> By looking to Jesus Like Him thou shalt be;
> Thy friends in thy conduct His likeness shall see.
>   —George C. Stephens

Prayer

We thank Thee, our heavenly Father, for the advantages and the authority which come from being able to spend quality time with You. Thank You for the invitation to meditate and concentrate on the good things which only You can provide. Thank You that Your Word teaches us how to turn a barren prayer vigil into a fruitful fellowship and a living relationship. May we never forget how to be still and know that You are God. In Jesus' name we pray. Amen.

—12—

PRAYING
PRIVATELY

The importance of prayer in the life of an individual and in the life of the corporate body of Christ cannot be overemphasized. Public praying and the unified supplication of large bodies of believers is recorded on numerous occasions in the Scriptures. Private, solitary appeals of man to God are also encouraged. "But thou, when thou prayest, enter into thy closet, and when thou has shut thy door, pray to thy Father which is in secret; and thy Father which seeth in secret shall reward thee openly" (Matthew 6:6). *The Living Bible* exclaims, "Go away by yourself, all alone and shut the door behind you and pray to your Father secretly." Please note that while the praying is done privately, the rewarding takes place openly!

To introduce this study, let's consider the proposition of privacy. Only a few years ago some of us had more privacy than we desired. We actually craved for times of social interaction, the crowd, the group, the festival and the mass celebration. Now there is very little or no privacy to be had by any individual in our society.

Privacy means "the state of being apart from company or observation." It is a cry for seclusion from the noise, the din, the push and shove of our competitive lifestyle. To be private is to be apart from, exclusive, not common or general but special. Privacy means "freedom from interference, freedom to grow, experience, and to control areas of your life without the imposition of others." In many ways privacy could be our first line of defense for numerous freedoms that are being subtly stolen by technology and other so-called forms of social progress.

The clamor of an overpopulated planet is for "breathing space"—somewhere an individual can be alone, on his own, undisturbed, unmolested and inviolable. The invasion of privacy is a serious matter. Many realize the crowded maze of our minds, our space and our lives. Whatever happened to that other world where we used to live? The one where we could wade the creek and the water was clear and unpolluted, stroll across the meadow and pick wild flowers for Mom, lie down on the hillside and chew on a blade of grass while staring up into a blue sky? And whatever happened to back porches with swings and front porches with rocking chairs?

The recent news of terrorism and hostages and the worldwide monitoring of nations for arms control tells us there is very little privacy in the new world order. Rapid transportation, hi-tech communications and the computerization of everything from robots to automobiles and pocket calculators has opened up a totally new Pandora's box for man to explore. A "spy in the sky" listens in on the world's communications while infrared cameras capture the action and satellite dishes transmit, collect and assimilate the data. It is therefore probable that the only true privacy most sincere souls will ever be able to enjoy is that spiritual paradise of spending personal, private, quiet time with God, and God alone, in prayer.

Sweet hour of prayer! sweet hour of prayer!
That calls me, from a world of care,
And bids me, at my Father's throne,
Make all my wants and wishes known;
In seasons of distress and grief,
My soul has often found relief,
And oft escaped the tempter's snare
By thy return, sweet hour of prayer.
   —W.W. Walford and William B. Bradbury

Have you ever been in a situation where you knew there was no privacy at all and everything you did was known by whoever wanted to know? This was at least the way I felt when the Ministers Trio, in which I sang, visited Moscow and Leningrad, Russia, on the way back from our servicemen's retreat in Berchtesgaden, Germany. We stayed in a hotel across from Red Square. *Life* magazine had featured it on their front cover, calling it the "Comrade Hilton." It was the newest and best in this capital city, and we were grateful to be able to stay there. It was not, however, a Hilton. Throughout our brief tour, which was tremendously enlightening, we each had the feeling that someone was watching every move we made and listening to every word spoken.

This extreme illustration of no privacy, which is experienced in many places in our world, is used to point out the priceless privilege of secret prayer. Prayer is a hot line to heaven. You and I have our own built-in "red telephone" with a personal, direct line into the throne room of God that the devil cannot horn in on or disconnect.

Look at four things: (1) some attitudes about solitude, (2) the need we all have to be alone, (3) the aptitude of solitude and (4) the quietude of solitude.

Attitudes About Solitude

Some of us are very open, social, outgoing, transparent and extroverted. Others are just the opposite. How I envy them! They are so private, reserved, almost reclusive and introverted. Then there are the middle-of-the-road types. They tell us the well-balanced individual can handle either type and keep it in perspective, though I'm not sure the experts have agreed on a definition for *well-balanced*. In my brief studies on the life of Christ, I have observed that Jesus was an individual who could be at home in the multitude or in solitude, in the city or the country, in a crowd or in the privacy of two. After ascending the stairwell of an old inner-city St. Louis church where one teacher stood teaching one little boy, I understood what the pastor meant when he said, "Jesus preached some of His greatest sermons to an audience of one." Jesus was not uncomfortable even on a one-to-one encounter. Jesus often sought for solitude and times of privacy when He and His heavenly Father could be together, all alone, just the two of them.

John 4:4 records how Jesus *needed* to go through Samaria. He undoubtedly needed to be alone and needed to meet the woman at Jacob's well. Jesus, therefore, sent His disciples ahead into the city to buy something to eat. While Jesus was seated in solitude, one very unhappy, confused and hopeless woman came out from the city to draw water. Many of you remember the story. Through a personal, private, one-on-one encounter, an entire city was brought to a saving knowledge of Jesus Christ.

"Jesus was led up of the spirit into the wilderness to be tempted of the devil. And when he had fasted forty days and forty nights, he was afterward an hungred" (Matthew 4:1, 2). The 40 days and nights of fasting and praying alone in the wilderness under the guidance and power of the Holy Spirit preserved Jesus from the most horrendous temptation ever devised for mortal man. Jesus met and overcame every point of Satan's strategy. Some things in life cannot be done corporately; they must be handled individually.

"He [Jesus] was praying in a certain place" (Luke 11:1). In other words, He was alone. When He finished praying, His disciples met Him with the request, "Lord, teach us to pray." The ancient phenomenon of prayer seemed to take on new meaning when exercised by Jesus. It was something more than form, ritual and routine. It was now life and breath, personal and real. Prayer was a spiritual essential.

In the Garden of Gethsemane, Jesus asked His disciples to watch and wait for Him while He went apart from them to a solitary place of quietude and privacy. When He returned, they had not identified with Him but were asleep. Jesus went alone to a place apart to pray in the Garden of Gethsemane. It was a tremendously agonizing time for the Son of God. It was a matter He had to handle alone, with the aid of His heavenly Father. There will be many times in life when no one will be able to help except God. When it happens, don't be afraid. Call on Him. He's just a prayer away.

The Need to Be Alone
I enjoy people. My mother took me to church when I was an infant. I attended Sunday school and sat on cane-bottomed chairs in the classroom before my feet could touch the floor. I sang my first song on radio at age 7 or 8 and started traveling in church work at age 11. How I wish I had kept a diary and made a record of all the churches we have visited, the people we have met and the homes in which we have stayed!

Our children are also very personable. It is rare for any of us to meet a stranger. Yet there are times when I desire to be alone. I need to be alone. I crave solitude. I am like a bear in the winter, driven by nature and circumstances to hibernation. There are other times when I desire to be with my wife and family. There are times in all of our lives when privacy, quietness and only the most significant together-ness is very important. I think the Scriptures bear this out, especially in the ministry of prayer. Far too many of us are burned out and burned up because we have not taken the time to be alone with ourselves and with our God. Did He not say in Exodus 20:3, "Thou shalt have no other gods before me"? Nothing—no person, place or thing—must deprive us of our exclusive time with God.

This word *alone* means "apart from other people." I think this must have been what happened to Jacob in Genesis 32:24: "And Jacob was left alone." It was 20 years after he had cheated Esau out of his birthright. All of this time the pressure had been mounting as Esau had become a strong leader and his tribe a large group. Now it was on the calendar. The time and place had been set for Jacob and Esau to meet face-to-face. Yes, the pressure was on! In order to cope with this kind of pressure, the kind that had been characterized by 20 years of wrong doing, 20 years of living under a cloud of guilt, experiencing the daily gnawing pain of conscience, Jacob had to have some help!

The Bible says he was left alone. During his solitude he encountered an angel. He wrestled with the angel. Many think the real encounter Jacob had was with himself. I think the problem was not so much Esau as it was Jacob. The only way for Jacob to handle Esau was to first handle Jacob. The best way to handle any problem is to seek God. Sure, he wrestled with an angel, but once he got Jacob in hand, he was able to handle Esau or whatever else needed to be handled.

The same thing happens to us. There are times when we need to be alone. Any problem or crisis that seems to be too much can be handled only after we get ourselves under control. Then, and only then, are we capable of handling anything we encounter. The reason is simply because we have the equipment and help of Almighty God.

"He that ruleth his spirit [is better] than he that taketh a city" (Proverbs 16:32).

In Exodus 3 you will begin to see the tremendous transition Moses went through from Pharaoh's house to the back side of the desert. The Bible says that he was actually caring for sheep. While there alone, in one of the most remote areas, Moses saw a bush suddenly catch on fire. Now it was not unusual for a bush to catch on fire in the desert. It would be very simple for a dry bush, because of spontaneous combustion, to suddenly light up and disappear in smoke. The only thing different about this particular bush was that it was not consumed. It would not burn up. So it kept on glowing and flaming until Moses ventured over to see what was happening. A voice spoke out of the bush saying, "Moses, take off your shoes, for the ground on which you stand is holy ground." Moses was having a personal, private confrontation with his Sovereign Creator. The omnipotent One! We are somewhat like Moses, it sometimes takes the back side of the desert to ignite our own personal burning bush and have God explain how we ought to act while standing on holy ground.

In Luke 9:18 Jesus was praying alone. Then He asked His disciples, "Whom say the people that I am?" Was He struggling with His self-image, His personal image or His public image? No! He wanted to know the spiritual perception of the people. In verse 36 after the transfiguration experience and the intervention of the voice of God, Jesus was once again "found alone." Almost every time men of the Word experienced important events, somewhere in their story you find the term *alone*. They were alone! Thus, we see the need for all of us to spend time alone with God.

The Aptitude of Solitude

Is there really an aptitude about solitude? *Aptitude* means "apt, that which we learn from something." In most situations an apt person will ask, "What is the purpose of it?" "What is apt to happen?" "What will normally and automatically come forth from it?" Yes, most of us can find an aptitude in the concept of solitude!

"Enter into thy closet, and shut the door" (Matthew 6:6). Shut the door and shut the world out. Shut the door and shut yourself in. The Ladies of Lee recently recorded this spiritual in the Forward in Faith studios:

> Shut the door, keep out the devil.
> Shut the door, keep the devil in the night.
> Shut the door, keep out the devil.
> Light the candle, everything's all right.

The closer we are to God, the further away from the world we become. The more time we spend with God, the less time we will spend with the things contrary to God. The more of God we possess, the more impact we will have on a gainsaying world. The reason for much drifting and spiritual instability, the reason for coldness of heart and lukewarmness of soul, the reason for lack of spiritual power is the lack of close fellowship and communion with God. To be anemic and malnourished spiritually is not the fault of someone else. It is our own fault. Each one of us is responsible for our own spiritual well-being. The best way to maintain a strong relationship with ourselves, our fellow-man and even our enemies is to maintain a strong relationship with God. When there is a weak horizontal relationship, it is an indication of a weak vertical relationship. When we consciously shut the door in order to maintain that priceless privacy and sacred secrecy, we not only shut the world out, we also shut ourselves in with God.

Think of It! Alone, You and God

It's private. It's secret. It's confidential, highly confidential. The song "Tell It to Jesus Alone" asks:

Are you weary? Are you heavy-hearted?
Tell it to Jesus, Tell it to Jesus,
Are you grieving over joys departed?
Tell it to Jesus alone.

Do the tears flow down your cheeks unbidden?
Have you sins that to man's eyes are hidden?
Do you fear the gath'ring clouds of sorrow?
Are you anxious what shall be tomorrow?

Tell it to Jesus, Tell it to Jesus.
He is a friend that's well known.
You have no other such a friend or brother;
Tell it to Jesus alone.
                —J.E. Rankin and E.S. Lorenz

Another classic chorus expresses the same idea in these terms:

Tell it to Jesus, He understands.
Burdens will leave you at His command
While you hold His guiding hand.
Tell it to Jesus, He understands.
                —D.M. Shanks

It's different when someone's listening, isn't it? I suppose most of our prayers are prayed when someone we know is listening. I've discovered we often do things a little differently when someone is present or someone is listening. When we pray in the presence of another person, we don't have that anonymity and protection. We sometimes put on airs and polish things up a little bit.

One Sunday morning I was out in the audience with my remote microphone, having a nice down-home, friendly, fireside chat with all the good saints in the sanctuary. Would you believe, when I was back on the platform, sitting comfortably in my pulpit chair, the minister of music sent me a note saying, "Pastor, are you aware that we are broadcasting *live* on the radio today?" Well, yes, I knew; and yes, I had forgotten. It does make a difference if you think someone is listening! We found out later that the engineer had forgotten to plug us in. Many times we think folks are listening when really they are not listening at all. We would be way ahead to just be ourselves at all times.

When it's just you and God, it's private, it's secret, it's highly confidential. You can open up and pour it all out just like it is. That's the wonderful thing about someone you feel comfortable with. Someone has said everyone needs a friend they can trust, a good close friend whom they love and who loves them, someone who can take whatever you pour out, the wheat and chaff together, someone who will take it in their hands and look it over, then with the breath of kindness blow the chaff away and keep only the wheat, the pure grain. That's what happens with our heavenly Father. We can freely, honestly and openly pour it all out to Him. *Lord, teach us to pray privately! Teach us to go into our closet, and teach us to shut the door.*

While some confession is public, most of it is private and very confidential. There must be a feeling of secrecy and trustworthiness which come when we understand it's just us and God. Then we are free to confess, to put it all into words. We are free to tell someone. How soothing and therapeutic it is sometimes just to say so! Tell it; share it. Allowing someone else to help you carry it seems to lighten the load.

One of the books in my library is titled *The Awesome Power of the Listening Ear.* I understand the best counselors are often those who know how to listen. That's why some of our parents, grandparents and best friends are such great counselors. They know how to listen empathetically and sympathetically.

What a fantastic quality!

For some time now Helen and I have been planning to record a duet album. I've recorded a number of solo albums and group albums but never one with just the two of us. One of the songs we have planned goes like this:

> There are times when I know not when,
> Nor where, nor what to do.
> If I only had someone I could talk to.
> Could it be that possibly I might get through to Him,
> To Jesus my friend, to talk now and then?
>
> I need somebody to tell my troubles to.
> Lord, could I please tell them to you?
> You always listen and know just what to do
> When I need somebody to tell my troubles to.
> —Bennie S. Triplett

Private prayer builds an inner defense against outside pressure. No area of life is immune from the subtle, unsuspecting attacks of Satan. Private prayer reinforces your defenses, keeps you on a 24-hour alert and equips you for the journey, regardless of the terrain. Private prayer not only strengthens your inner defenses against would-be pressures and peer groups, it also gives you a better view and an overall perspective. A man on his knees is taller in many respects than most men on their feet or even on their tiptoes. The view from God's throne is much clearer than the view from the pit or the gutter.

"But they that wait upon the Lord shall renew their strength; they shall mount up with wings as eagles; they shall run, and not be weary; and they shall walk, and not faint" (Isaiah 40:31). God wants us to stand up and spread our wings. He wants us to soar, to rise up above the routine and the mundane. God has plans for you. God's presence is accompanied by His power.

Strength comes from personal, spiritual relationships. "And when thou hast shut thy door." So many forget to shut the door and as a result are vulnerable. Their whole house and all of their privileges are vulnerable. Shutting the door procures privacy. Shutting the door secures safety. Shutting the door insures intimacy. "Pray to the Father." Prayer is a privileged relationship. Prayer is a family relationship. It has to do with a father and his children, with sons and daughters, elder brothers and sisters and their parents. There are no greater ties, stronger bonds nor more enduring affinity than that of a son to his father, a mother to her daughter and a daughter to her mother, of a husband to his wife and a wife to her husband. No other relationship can be compared to these. The purest, most supportive strength comes to each of us from these exclusive relationships.

Private communication builds unspeakable confidence. There is nothing like being on the inside of things, getting our information straight from the original source. During the hostage crisis in Iran, President Jimmy Carter and his wife, Rosalyn, called the families of the hostages to a special gathering. One shot of the television camera showed the president whispering into the ear of one of the wives. Later in the interview the report was given, "My husband has been released. He will arrive in Germany in the morning." Word from an authoritative source builds irrefutable confidence. Of course, we enjoy getting letters, bulletins, telegrams, messages and even telephone calls. No manner of communication, however, is comparable to a face-to-face, heart-to-heart union which comes from being together, just you and someone very special. Private communication builds confidence.

The Quietude of Solitude

"Pray to thy Father which is in secret; and thy Father which seeth in secret shall reward thee openly." There is a quietude in solitude. There is a peace, a calmness, an assurance and a reassurance which comes from the presence of a significant other. At Christ's arrival in Bethlehem, the angels sang, "On earth peace, good will toward men" (Luke 2:14). At His word a tempestuous sea subsided and went to sleep with His, "Peace be still" (Mark 4:39). "Peace be unto you" was His greeting to the private gathering of disciples behind closed doors, after His crucifixion and resurrection (John 20:19, 21, 26). To the sick and incurable He says, "Go in peace and be whole of thy plague" (Mark 5:34). To the guilty and unsaved He says, "Thy faith hath saved thee; go in peace" (Luke 7:50). To the whole world the scriptures exhort, "Be anxious for nothing, but in everything by prayer and supplication with thanksgiving let your requests be made known to God; and the peace of God which surpasses all understanding will guard your hearts and minds through Christ Jesus" (Philippians 4:6, 7, *NKJV*).

Private prayer ministers wholeness to the sincere suppliant. The word *keep* in Philippians 4:7 means "to guard" and "to garrison." It is as if God, by His Holy Spirit, turns the power of peace into an army or battalion of soldiers and lines them up around your heart, so as to protect it from the fiery darts of the enemy. Then He sends another battalion of special forces to guard your mind from any intrusion or subversion. When the peace of God keeps you, there is no security nor serenity that can compare. There is a quietude in God's solitude. It is not only enjoyed in secret, it is also enjoyed in superabundance. "He shall reward thee openly."

Shut in with God, in a secret place.
There in the spirit, beholding His face.

165

Gaining new power, to run in this race.
O, I love to be shut in with God.
        —William Grum

Prayer

Thank You, our heavenly Father, for allowing us the privilege of praying privately. Oh, thou God of the universe and God of the ages, condescending from heaven to earth to tabernacle in human flesh, to be with us and to be one of us, how we relish and cherish the thought of Thee, and especially the thought of being with Thee in solitude. Make us more mindful of Thee so that we may be more like Thee. This we pray in Jesus' name. Amen.

CHAPTER
—13—

PRAYING
PATIENTLY

Someone has said, "God answers prayer in one of three ways: sometimes He says, 'Yes!'; sometimes He says, 'No!'; and sometimes He says, 'Wait a while!'" We will examine the third concept in "Praying Patiently." This verse sums it up: "I waited patiently for the Lord; and he inclined unto me, and heard my cry" (Psalm 40:1).

Patience is "forbearance, long-suffering and constancy." It means bearing or enduring pain and trials without complaining. It means the exercise of forbearance under provocation, expectancy with calmness and without discontent. Sometimes we get so psyched up and anxious over things, we have a hard time controlling ourselves, keeping our cool and staying calm. If things don't go exactly as we planned, it is not time for panic but rather for patience.

Patience means being undisturbed by obstacles, delays and failures. It means persevering and continuing before the Lord. It is that perfecting grace which helps to sculpt us and mold us into the image of the Lord Jesus Christ. We are able to look to Him as our example and strive to exercise the same patient endurance that He exhibited in His life and ministry.

In learning patience in prayer there are three areas to study: (1) the regimentation of patient prayer (2) the requirements of patient prayer, and (3) the rewards of patient prayer. *Lord, teach us to pray patiently!*

The Regimentation of Patient Prayer

Learning to Deal Patiently With Ourselves

The first thing we encounter in the regimentation of praying patiently is ourselves. We must all learn to deal with our ownselves on a continuing basis. We must learn to exercise patience and control while coping with each circumstance we face. Most of us are normal human beings, and this means we are not always in tune with the cadence and timing of God. Usually we either run ahead or lag behind; seldom are we in step with God.

If I knew Grandpa Freeman was going to town, I'd get so excited thinking about the candy at the grocery store that I would run ahead, dancing, jumping and burning myself out the first block or so. Then I'd lag behind, crying for Grandpa to wait for me or come get me. I had not learned to pace myself and control my excitement and enthusiasm.

Many times we behave this way concerning the important things of God. We have a hard time pacing ourselves, keeping in step, being consistent and considerate. We have difficulty maintaining that steady, unwavering patience we need rather than the hot and cold extremes of running ahead or lagging behind. Are we so programmed religiously that only certain things turn us on and get us excited? As a result, we spend all our energy on our desires and miss God's requirements. How easy it is to major in minors and minor in majors. We get so caught up in the XYZs we forget the basic ABCs. There is no way in the Christian experience to abort, abandon and leapfrog God's basics—they are primary and essential.

It reminds me of our son, Steve, when he was growing up. During a trip we stopped at a nice restaurant in Chattanooga to eat breakfast. After reading the menus, we began to order ham and eggs, grits, and so forth. The waitress looked over at Steve and said, "Son, what will you have? Steve replied, "I'll have a Milky Way and a Coke."

That's the way we are oftentimes. We like the things which we like. Don't mention a balanced diet; don't bother us with the things we need. We'll get to that later. How easy it is to miss the essentials because we are so enamored with incidentals. It's like going downhill; it's so easy, we can coast. We don't have to think or use much energy, so we run ahead—faster and faster. Pretty soon things get out of control, and we know what eventually happens. The Lord has to pick us up, dust us off, hold our hand, slow us down and steady our pace.

Prayer teaches us to take each step as God takes it, not running ahead or lagging behind. Of course we get tired, and with a lack of concentration, we get out of cadence. Then when something exciting happens, we rush to get in on it, suddenly realizing that we're too late and are unprepared because we're out of breath. How sad it is to be unable or incapable of getting involved. That's what happens when we fail to prepare and equip ourselves properly for Christian service. When the opportunities come, we are unable to take advantage of them. *Lord, teach us to regiment ourselves by praying for patience.*

Do we indeed have more problems with ourselves than anyone else? Yes, as the sign reads which sits on the bookshelf of my study, "Lord, give me patience . . . but hurry up!" The consistent, step-by-step, one day at a time approach can be very important to the child of God.

We sometimes experience what I call "sanctified impatience" or "holy discontent." We need to understand that God is in the whirlwind, but He is also in the still, small voice. God is leading in the cloud by day as well as the fire by night. Sometimes we need to "stand still and see the salvation of the Lord" (Exodus 14:13). Prayer teaches us the patient acceptance and regimentation of ourselves.

Learning to Deal Patiently With Others

We need patience in dealing with others. Sometimes the lack of concern for others can really frustrate us. Then again, too much involvement with others can be just as disturbing.

How many times in our anxiety to do something, we do too much, too little or we are not sure what we ought to do? As one has exclaimed, "Sometimes we are as tactful as a bull in a china shop." Dale Carnegie warns, "If you're going to gather honey, don't turn over the hive."

"And be ye kind one to another, tenderhearted, forgiving one another, even as God for Christ's sake hath forgiven you" (Ephesians 4:32). *The Living Bible* says, "Stop being mean, bad-tempered, and angry. Quarreling, harsh words, and dislike of others should have no place in your lives. Instead, be kind to each other, tenderhearted, forgiving one another, just as God has forgiven you because you belong to Christ" (vv. 31, 32). "Better is the end of a thing than the beginning thereof: and the patient in spirit is better than the proud in spirit" (Ecclesiastes 7:8).

In the parable of the sower, Jesus describes the good soil as "an honest and good heart, having heard the word, keep it, and bring forth fruit with patience" (Luke 8:15). "Labor not for the meat which perisheth, but for that meat which endureth" (John 6:27). James speaks of Christian testing and the purpose of testing: "Knowing this, that the trying of your faith worketh patience. But let patience have her perfect work, that ye may be perfect and entire, wanting nothing" (James 1:3, 4). *The Living Bible* says, "Dear brothers, is your life full of difficulties and temptations? Then be happy, for when the way is rough, your patience has a chance to grow. So let it grow, and don't try to squirm out of your problems. For when your patience is finally in full bloom, then you will be ready for anything, strong in character, full and complete" (James 1:2-4). "Be patient therefore, brethren . . . . Behold, the husbandman waiteth for the precious fruit of the earth, and hath long patience for it" (James 5:7).

Paul talks about a blameless and approved ministry. "Ministers of God, in much patience" (2 Corinthians 6:4). "We . . . glory in you . . . for your patience and your faith" (2 Thessalonians 1:4). "Oh, Timothy, you are God's man. Run from all these evil things and work instead at what is right and good, learning to trust him and love others, and to be patient and gentle" (1 Timothy 6:11, *TLB*). "But thou hast fully known my . . . patience" (2 Timothy 3:10). "That the aged men be . . . sound . . . in patience" (Titus 2:2). Peter's spiritual equation calls for the adding "to our temperance, patience; and to your patience, godliness" (2 Peter 1:6). "For if these things be in you, and abound, they make you that ye shall neither be barren nor unfruitful in the knowledge of our Lord Jesus Christ" (2 Peter 1:8). "Be not slothful, but followers of them who through faith and patience inherit the promises" (Hebrews 6:12).

Learning to Deal Patiently With God
How we need patience in accepting the providence and the wisdom of God. Like children, we are so used to wanting things our way and no other way—everything done according to our design and for our reasons. Sometimes God has no alternative but to teach us that He does things in His own time. God is sovereign!

God not only does things in His own time but also in his own way. Can you imagine what kind of ark we would have built? Do you suppose we would have preserved all of the species? What kind of object lesson would science have arranged for Jonah as a means of convincing him to get ready to hold revival in Nineveh? Can you imagine what kind of transportation we would have arranged for Mary, Joseph and Jesus to escape to Egypt and flee the wrath of Herod, or upon which animal Christ should ride for His triumphal entry into the Holy City of Jerusalem? God does things in His own time and in His own way. Rest assured also that His way is the right way.

God does things for His own immutable purposes. With our finite minds there is no way for us to see the things God sees and to know the things God knows. This is why we must thrust ourselves upon His all-seeing, all-knowing, all-wise, understanding love and trust Him implicitly.

"And we know that all things work together for good to them that love God, to them who are the called according to his purpose" (Romans 8:28).

"I am Alpha and Omega, the beginning and the end, the first and the last" (Revelation 22:13).

He knows the end from the beginning and the beginning from the end. He is working all things for our good. Once we understand this, we should rest and relax in His care. The Bible teaches us to wait patiently upon the Lord, turn everything over to Him and trust Him. Prayer gives us the patience to trust an all-wise, ever-present and all-powerful God. *Lord, teach us to pray patiently!*

The Requirements of Patient Prayer

Patience Requires Endurance

One of the requirements of patience is listed in Luke 21:19, "In your patience possess ye your souls."

By patient endurance we keep our souls in harmony with God. The constancy remains. We are not sporadic, erratic and spasmodic. The crying need of the 20th century is for consistent, hour-by-hour, day-by-day, month-by-month, year-by-year and life-by-life commitments to God.

Far too many are like an elevator spiritually—"up and down, up and down." We are either floating around on a pink cloud, picking a golden harp, or we are pulling a subsoil plow trying to undermine China. We are either on the mountaintop or in the valley. Somewhere and somehow there must be a consistency, a steadiness and a steadfastness. Christians don't have to go around with a north-and-south look on their faces instead of an east-and-west. We don't have to look like we've been chewing on a dill pickle, sleeping under a crab apple tree and eating cream out of a churn. Many have seen prettier pictures on iodine bottles (a crossbones and a skull with the warning—POISON).

The Christian life doesn't have to be up-and-down or erratic. The Christian life can be patient, "stedfast, unmoveable, always abounding in the work of the Lord" (1 Corinthians 15:58).

One day while out west visiting the Yellowstone National Park, our family was standing in front of a famous lodge. Seeing many people gathering at a certain place in a field out in front of the lodge, I questioned in my mind what was going on. The crowd was getting bigger and bigger. I noticed they kept looking at their watches. Helen, the children and I took seats. The man sitting next to me said, "It'll just be a couple more seconds." Then all of a sudden, the ground began to vibrate and rumble. Out of the ground in the middle of the open field in front of us came a tall column of hot steam and water that shot high into the sky. Cameras had already been aimed and adjusted. They knew exactly how high it would go. They knew its velocity;

and sure enough, it stayed up for just a short period and then came right back down.

I had my camera and got a picture also. I asked someone, "What do they call this?" And one gentleman said to me, "That's Old Faithful!" It had been doing this for a long time. Old Faithful! You could count on it. It was always there. You could almost set your watch by it. Some had even ventured to measure it. It was constant, consistent and always on time. Patience indeed requires endurance.

Patience Requires Experience

"We glory in tribulations also: knowing that tribulation worketh patience; and patience, experience; and experience, hope: and hope maketh not ashamed; because the love of God is shed abroad in our hearts by the Holy Ghost which is given unto us" (Romans 5:3-5).

Do tribulations work patience? Yes, the Bible says we glory in tribulations! Isn't it wonderful that we have the Bible? Patience requires experience, and experience teaches us a lot of good lessons for life.

Patience Requires Emptying Out and Getting Rid Of

"Wherefore seeing we also are compassed about with so great a cloud of witnesses, let us lay aside every weight, and the sin which doth so easily beset us, and let us run with patience the race that is set before us" (Hebrews 12:1).

We need to get rid of anything that is hindering our Christian progress. Whatever has taken first place in our life we need to replace with Jesus Christ because He ought to have first place in our life. We need to look "unto Jesus, the author and finisher of our faith" (Hebrews 12:2). Patience requires a moving out and a moving in.

Patience Requires an Example

"Behold, we count them happy which endure. Ye have heard of the patience of Job" (James 5:11).

Many beautiful role models exemplifying Jesus Christ are given to us by the Holy Spirit. Is it any wonder the disciples asked Jesus to teach them to pray? And should we not join them by saying, "Lord, teach us to pray patiently"?

The Reward of Patience

The Reward of Patience Is Salvation

"I have waited for thy salvation, O Lord" (Genesis 49:18).

"Truly my soul waiteth upon God: from Him cometh my salvation" (Psalm 62:1).

You remember Simeon. When the baby Jesus was brought by Mary and Joseph to the temple, this elderly prophet held the Christ child in his arms because he had been waiting for "the consolation of Israel" (Luke 2:25). Listen! "Lord, now lettest thou thy servant depart in peace, . . . for mine eyes have seen thy salvation" (Luke 2:29, 30). What patience this man of God must have possessed in order to experience this momentous occasion!

The Reward of Patience Is Knowledge

Instruction comes from waiting on the Lord.

"Shew me thy ways, O Lord; teach me thy paths. Lead me in thy truth, and teach me: for thou art the God of my salvation; on thee do I wait all the day" (Psalm 25:4, 5).

The Reward of Patience Is the Abundance of God's Blessings

Blessings come to those who wait on the Lord.

"Let none that wait on thee be ashamed" (Psalm 25:3).

"Let integrity and uprightness preserve me; for I wait on thee" (Psalm 25:21).

"Wait on the Lord: be of good courage, and he shall strengthen thine heart: wait, I say, on the Lord" (Psalm 27:14).

"Rest in the Lord, and wait patiently for him: fret not thyself because of him who prosperth in his way, because of the man who bringeth wicked devices to pass" (Psalm 37:7).

"For since the beginning of the world men have not heard, nor perceived by the ear, neither hath the eye seen, O God, beside thee, what he hath prepared for him that waiteth for him" (Isaiah 64:4).

"Eye hath not seen, nor ear heard, neither have entered into the heart of man, the things which God hath prepared for them that love him" (1 Corinthians 2:9).

"Behold, I send the promise of my Father upon you: but tarry ye in the city of Jerusalem, until ye be endued with power from on high" (Luke 24:49).

"And, being assembled together with them, commanded them that they should not depart from Jerusalem, but wait for the promise of the Father, which, saith he, ye have heard of me, for John truly baptized with water; but ye shall be baptized with the Holy Ghost not many days hence" (Acts 1:4, 5).

Waiting and praying patiently brings multiple blessings.

"I waited patiently for the Lord; and he inclined unto me, and heard my cry. He brought me up also out of a horrible pit, out of the miry clay, and set my feet upon a rock, and established my goings. And he hath put a new song in my mouth, even praise unto our God" (Psalm 40:1-3).

Let's review the list again: He turned toward me. He

inclined Himself in my direction. He heard me. He plucked me up out of the pit of perdition. He pulled me from the muck and mire of corruption. He planted me on a solid foundation when He put my feet on the rock. He established my goings. He set the sail of my ship and arranged for a rudder that would properly steer my course.   He orchestrated it and accompanied it with music when He put a song in my mouth, even praise unto our God.

> God teach me to be patient;
> Teach me to go slow—
> Teach me how to "wait on You"
> When my way I do not know . . . Teach
> me how to quiet
> My racing, rising heart
> So I may hear the answer
> You are trying to impart . . . Teach
> me to let go, dear God,
> And pray undisturbed until
> My heart is filled with inner peace,
> And I learn to know Your will.
>   —Helen Steiner Rice

How impatient we are with God, and how patient He is with us! The parable of the unmerciful servant in Matthew 18:23-25 graphically portrays the dichotomy. Be pleased, O wayward one, that you are accountable to Jesus Christ— the loving, kind, merciful and patient Savior of the world— rather than to any man who might set himself up as your judge and jury.

Conclusion
In closing this study on the privilege of intercessory prayer, I want to share a beautiful story told by Merv Rosele in his book *Challenging Youth for Christ*.

Little Mary was taken with a sudden illness. When her father arrived home from work, he rushed her to the emergency room of the nearest hospital. Mary's mother was bedfast and had been ill for some time. Her father was not a Christian but loved his family very much. After examining her, the doctor said to Mary's father, "To save the life of your daughter, we will need to perform surgery immediately." Explaining the surgical procedure to Mary, he introduced her to a nurse who would prepare her for the operation.

"Did you say I would have to go to sleep, doctor?" Mary asked.

"Oh, yes," he explained, "We always put folks to sleep before we operate."

"Well," said Mary, "I suppose if I'm going to go to sleep, I ought to say my prayers."

He looked around from the nurse to Mary and her father. The doctor had never encountered a circumstance such as this. So he said to Mary reassuringly, "Why of course, my dear, if you would like to say your prayers, go right ahead!"

And so, right then and there, before the doctor, the nurse and her father in the emergency room of the large hospital, little Mary bowed her head. Adjusting the long golden locks of hair around her shoulders, she closed her eyelids over those shiny blue eyes. Touching the tips of her fingers underneath the dimple in her chin, Mary began to pray. "Oh, Jesus, You know where I am, and You know that Mommy is home, sick in bed. Bless dear Papa, this surgeon, his nurse, my Sunday school teacher and all. For Your sake. Amen!"

Her father couldn't take it any longer; he rushed down the hall to the chapel where he surrendered his heart to Christ. Little Mary came through the operation with flying colors. Her mother got well, and her Sunday school class continued to grow. All because when it came time to pray, a little girl knew what to do and how to do it. *Lord, teach us to pray!*

Prayer

   For Thine is the kingdom, the power and the glory, forever and ever! Amen!